The Pianist's Guide to Historic Improvisation

John J. Mortensen

OXFORD
UNIVERSITY PRESS

OXFORD
UNIVERSITY PRESS

Oxford University Press is a department of the University of Oxford. It furthers the University's objective of excellence in research, scholarship, and education by publishing worldwide. Oxford is a registered trade mark of Oxford University Press in the UK and certain other countries.

Published in the United States of America by Oxford University Press
198 Madison Avenue, New York, NY 10016, United States of America.

© Oxford University Press 2020

Library of Congress Cataloging-in-Publication Data
Names: Mortensen, John J., author.
Title: The pianist's guide to historic improvisation / John J. Mortensen.
Description: New York : Oxford University Press, 2020. |
Includes bibliographical references and index.
Identifiers: LCCN 2019047448 (print) | LCCN 2019047449 (ebook) |
ISBN 9780190920395 (hardback) | ISBN 9780190920401 (paperback) |
ISBN 9780190920425 (epub) | ISBN 9780190920432 (Online)
Subjects: LCSH: Improvisation (Music) | Piano—Instruction and study. |
Performance practice (Music)—History—18th century.
Classification: LCC MT68 .M617 2020 (print) | LCC MT68 (ebook) |
DDC 786.2/136—dc23
LC record available at https://lccn.loc.gov/2019047448
LC ebook record available at https://lccn.loc.gov/2019047449

9 8 7 6 5

Paperback printed by Marquis, Canada
Hardback printed by Bridgeport National Bindery, Inc., United States of America

The Pianist's Guide to Historic Improvisation

Contents

Acknowledgments

I started writing this book without knowing what I was talking about. I am therefore grateful to the musicians at the Cork School of Music in Ireland and the Jazeps Vitols Latvian Music Academy in Latvia for their dedication to the art of improvisation and for allowing me to learn while teaching. Dr. Gabriela Mayer of Cork and Dr. Toms Ostrovskis of Riga pulled strings and moved mountains to make visiting professorships at these schools possible.

Professor Beth Porter generously supported the sabbatical that helped this book exist. Dr. Charles R. Clevenger doubled his workload by taking on my American students for a semester just as he was about to retire. My friend and coconspirator in sundry schemes, he is a gentleman, a scholar, and a perfectly adequate pianist.

My beloved wife Linda cheered me along with equal parts enthusiasm, patience, and sympathy. She is a lioness who defends the vulnerable and frightens the wicked. I dedicate this book to her.

About the Companion Website

www.johnmortensen.com

The author has created a web page to accompany *The Pianist's Guide to Historic Improvisation*. Material that cannot be made available in a book is provided here, namely an online community for improvisers to discuss progress, post recordings, and interact with the author. The reader is encouraged to consult this resource in conjunction with the chapter[s].

Introduction

This book is for pianists who wish to improvise. Many will be experienced performers—perhaps even veteran concert artists—who are nevertheless beginners at improvisation. This contradiction is a reflection of our educational system. Those who attend collegiate music schools spend nearly all time and effort on learning, perfecting, and reciting masterpieces from the standard repertoire. As far as I can remember, no one ever taught or advocated for improvisation during my decade as a student in music schools. Certainly no one ever improvised anything substantial in a concert (except for the jazz musicians, who were, I regret to say, a separate division and generally viewed with complete indifference by the classical community). Nor did any history professor mention that long ago, improvisation was commonplace and indeed an indispensable skill for much of the daily activity of a working musician.

I continue to dedicate a portion of my career to perfecting and reciting masterpieces of the repertoire, and teaching my students to do the same. That tradition is dear to me. Still, if I have one regret about my traditional education, it's that it wasn't traditional enough. We have forgotten that in the eighteenth century—those hundred years that form the bedrock of classical music—improvisation was a foundation of music training. Oddly, our discipline has discarded a practice that helped bring it into being. Perhaps it is time to retrieve it from the junk heap of history and give it a good dusting off.

I love the legends of the improvisational powers of the masters: Bach creating elaborate fugues on the spot, or Beethoven humiliating Daniel Steibelt by riffing upon and thereby exposing the weakness of the latter's inferior tunes. The stories implied that these abilities were instances of inexplicable genius which we could admire in slack-jawed wonder but never emulate. But that isn't right. Bach could improvise fugues not because he was unique but because almost any properly trained keyboard player in his day could. Even mediocre talents could improvise mediocre fugues. Bach was exceptionally good at something that pretty much everyone could do at a passable level. They could all do it because it was built into their musical thinking from the very beginning of their training.

Alas, it is not possible to go back and relive our training from the beginning. We must work with the abilities and habits of mind which our education has put in place. That is one reason that this book does not proceed in a strict historical order. If it did so, we would begin with simple, compound, and double cadences as the first order of business, but we will postpone that topic until Chapter 10 and use the reader's prior knowledge of cadences as a temporary measure. Our actual starting point will be the figuration prelude, a form of improvisation I believe is particularly accessible and rewarding to the modern pianist.

For similar reasons, discussions of harmony will take place in familiar, contemporary language at the beginning of the book, and gradually move to more historic terms later. Contemporary notions of analysis (in particular the use of Roman numerals and commercial chord symbols) do not represent eighteenth-century conceptions of music, in which a bass line gives rise to counterpointing voices ultimately combining in harmony. As a consequence of modern education, most readers will have a more complete grasp of harmony than of counterpoint. The reader already faces an arduous climb in learning to extemporize in old styles; asking for a sudden shift to a new mode of analysis may prove disheartening. For pedagogical reasons, then, I think it justifiable to use the reader's existing harmonic thought patterns (for a while) rather than discard them. Our terminology will flit blithely between figured bass, Roman analysis, and modern chord symbols. As the book proceeds, you will find fewer contemporary analytical references, and more authentic terminology from the eighteenth century. I am well aware that this approach is a compromise between the demands of authenticity and pedagogy, and (in this book, at least) I have decided in favor of pedagogy.

I chose certain kinds of pieces to improvise and dwell upon at length, while ignoring others. Again, pedagogical reasons stand behind this decision. In a work of theory or history, a reader may encounter a vast array of music literature, note what is important about each example, and move on. Not so with improvisation. Absolute mastery of every single detail, in real time, in many different keys, is indispensable. The reader must not only take in the material but absorb and rattle it off at will, while the metronome is clicking. Inevitably, this means many repetitions of limited material. With regret, then, some praiseworthy musical styles must go unmentioned. I will refer casually to the eighteenth century as the source of the music in this book, but at times may venture into the neighboring centuries in either direction.

This book rarely addresses the question of expressive playing because the mechanics of music—how it works and what you must know to create it yourself—could fill ten hefty tomes as it is. We already have our work cut out for us.

This is a method book—a volume of instruction and exercise. I certainly hope that you enjoy reading it, but reading alone will not be enough to turn you into an improviser. To gain mastery over the improvisational ideas presented here, you will need to devote significant time to practicing at the keyboard. The only place this book is useful is on the music rack of your piano.

I teach courses and workshops in classical improvisation at many colleges. Invariably, when I see an improvising student get stuck, it is because some fairly simple step has been neglected: the student isn't sure what key we are in right now, or can't remember the cadences we were supposed to memorize, or didn't learn Rule of the Octave thoroughly. Developing improvisational skill is like building a pyramid. The stones higher up stand upon those lower down, and the more the foundational stones have been perfectly squared and polished, the more stable the upper structure will be. Even a little bit of wobble among the stones at the base of a pyramid will result in terrifying, vertiginous instability at the top. Please practice each step very thoroughly, and if your improvisations seem to fall apart at some point, go back and find the stones that need to be polished and squared.

This is a book for beginning improvisers, but not for beginning musicians. In order to work through this material, the following abilities are required:

1. You need to read music for keyboard with moderate fluency. This book does not indulge in spectacular piano virtuosity, but you will have to play a tremendous variety of chords, scales, arpeggios, and figurations typical of the eighteenth century. You will need sufficient keyboard ability to play independent parts in each hand.

2. You need to have an education in music theory approximately equal to three semesters of college study. This will include Roman numeral analysis, figured bass, modern chord symbols, chord inversions, chord qualities (major, minor, diminished, etc.), secondary dominants, scales (major and all forms of the minor), and nonchord tones such as neighbors, suspensions, and passing tones. If you have not taken music theory courses, you can find excellent tutorials online, which provide the same material colleges teach.

3. Perhaps most importantly, you must transpose all the exercises as indicated. I am painfully aware how much students hate to transpose. They think transposing is difficult. In fact it is not difficult, but unfamiliar. Is it difficult to count to 100 in Japanese? Millions of small children can do it, so obviously it isn't difficult. But I can't, because it is unfamiliar to me. Initially, transposing will feel difficult because it will be unfamiliar. If you keep at it, you find that you will gain a marvelous familiarity with

all twenty-four keys. Once you gain the familiarity of transposition, it feels like a superpower.

4. You will need the patience to practice with a metronome. Even an otherwise advanced improvisation will sound depressingly bad with unstable rhythm. The ability to control tempo is crucial for all performers, of course, but for improvisers the power to pace the notes and not rush through them provides a little extra time to think about what to do next. I have often witnessed capable improvisers sabotaging things by rushing the tempo and depriving themselves of time to think. And, of course, I have done it myself!

In tandem with studying this book, you should keep a *zibaldone*. This Italian word means "heap of things" and refers to a personal notebook, sometimes known as a commonplace book. Robert Gjerdingen describes it as "a music student's notebook of exercises and rules" filled with "custom-tailored lessons." A zibaldone is a way of interacting with and making notes upon the world of improvisation. Whenever I come upon a particularly fine passage I wish to remember, I write it down in my zibaldone. I keep a table of handy tunes that work well for improvising fugues, a list of lovely sequences in various meters, my favorite ways of elaborating fauxbourdon progressions, and anything else that is worthwhile and useful for improvisation. I use a three-ring binder so I can add pages of manuscript paper at any location.

Writing by hand is slow and laborious, which is why it is so powerful: you will be forced into a sustained encounter with the material. I do not think it would be a good idea to use some trendy new app a keep a digital zibaldone on your phone. It's too easy and effortless to scoop up information through technology; everything goes in a folder and nothing goes in your head. This book includes many ideas for using your zibaldone to further your study.

While some readers will be part of a school or conservatory, others will be learning on their own. I believe that we learn better when surrounded by the encouragement of other people. For that reason I have created an online community where readers can discuss their learning process, access additional improvisation resources, and cheer one another on. Please visit www.johnmortensen.com to learn more.

Figuration Prelude

We begin improvisation with the figuration prelude because it consists only of a chord progression elaborated by a constant pattern of broken notes. If you understand the chords and can manage the figuration, you can make a piece of music. This chapter will guide you through the process of learning to create your own figuration preludes. You will encounter five techniques, each of which you will use to create a section of the prelude. The techniques in this chapter are openers, sequences, modulations, cadences, and endings.

Openers are chord progressions that work well to start improvisations. You will learn two. Sequences are musical patterns that rise or fall; you will learn one of each. Modulations move the music to another key, and you will learn four modulations. Cadences conclude one section and get you ready for the next. You will learn one cadence. Finally, you will learn two endings. Endings, obviously, go at the end.

Once you have mastered all these techniques, you will learn to use figuration, the decorative note patterns that turn plain chords into interesting music. When you put all these things together, you will be able to improvise complete figuration preludes in eighteenth-century style.

The Page One

Right now, improvise a story about a polar bear. If I asked you to do that, how would you begin? The other day I asked a student at a music workshop to tell a story on the spur of the moment. Although momentarily surprised by my request, the student came up with something like this: "Once upon a time, there was a polar bear who lived at the North Pole. One day she decided to take a long walk to see what was to the south. When she arrived in Canada, she met a Mountie on a horse . . ." And on it went. It was a good story.

We can all improvise stories, even when called upon suddenly, because we are fluent in our native language. But notice how we often begin with "Once upon a time." We could also use "One time" or "So I was walking down the street" or "What had happened was" or "Two guys walk into a bar" or "There once was" or "A long time ago in a galaxy far, far away." You have heard all these openers before. We use them to start stories because they signal to the audience that this is the beginning, they should start listening, and we are about to lay the groundwork of the story. Stories need openers, and we have many familiar ones that we use over and over. Music also needs openers, and happily, we have many and can use them over and over. Our first opener comes from J. S. Bach. Example 2.1 shows the first four bars of the Prelude in C from Book I of the *Well-Tempered Clavier* (WTC). Notice that it is really just a simple chord progression decorated with consistent figuration; that's what a figuration prelude is.

Go to the piano and play the example. Then remove the 16th-note figuration and figure out what the block chords would be. You should come up with Example 2.2. Take note of the harmonic analysis.

Now look at these other openers from Bach (Examples 2.3–2.8).

EXAMPLE 2.1   The Page One from J. S. Bach's *Well-Tempered Clavier*.

EXAMPLE 2.2   The Page One progression as block chords.

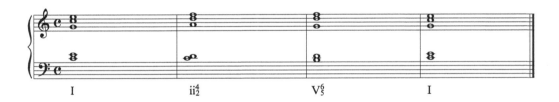

$$I \qquad ii^4_2 \qquad V^6_5 \qquad I$$

EXAMPLE 2.3   The Page One, J. S. Bach's Partita in E minor.

EXAMPLE 2.4   The Page One, J. S. Bach's Prelude in D minor, WTC I.

EXAMPLE 2.5   The Page One, J. S. Bach's Prelude in E-flat minor, WTC I.

EXAMPLE 2.6   The Page One, J. S. Bach's Prelude in E minor, ETC I.

EXAMPLE 2.7   The Page One, J. S. Bach's Prelude in G, WTC I.

EXAMPLE 2.8   The Page One (in both tonic and dominant), J. S. Bach's Prelude in A minor, WTC I.

All these openers use the same four basic chords, with only slight alterations. This progression is one of Bach's favorites. The Prelude in A minor (Example 2.8) even includes the progression twice in a row, once in the tonic and then in the dominant. Bach did not have a specific name for it, so we will call it Page One, since it opens the WTC. (The progression is by no means unique to Bach; we can find the same pattern in music of Mozart, Rameau, Fischer, Niedt, Vinci, Vanhal, Lully, and countless others.)

Let's Learn Page One Thoroughly

EXERCISE: Memorize the first four bars of the WTC I C major prelude. Play it as written, and as block chords as in Example 2.2. Transpose it to all 24 keys and figure out how you have to alter it for the minor mode. Try it starting with different chord tones on the top of the first chord. (When the root is in the soprano, the chord is in *first position*; the third in the soprano is *second position*, and the fifth in the soprano is *third position*. It is important to distinguish between position, which refers to the soprano, and inversion, which refers to the bass.) Now try it in three voices. The original has five, but we will often improvise with three. Can you create a version of the same progression in just three voices? (If you need help, look ahead to Example 2.11.) As a final challenge, try playing the Page One in all available positions of the chord.

Sequence: Descending 7-6

After you create an opener, you need another event so that your improvisation can continue. In eighteenth-century music, an easy way is to use a sequence. In a sequence every voice, rhythm, leap, and chord behaves according to a pattern. This makes it easy to extend the music because you only need to keep repeating the pattern. What's more, sequences sound interesting and beautiful. Our first sequence is the Descending 7-6.

The "7-6" refers to the dissonant-consonant pairs of intervals that make this sequence work. In eighteenth-century music, intervals of a seventh are considered dissonant, whereas sixths are consonant. They represent tension and release. Example 2.9 includes major and minor versions of the descending 7-6 sequence. The outer voices are where the 7-6 intervals occur. At some point you have to break the sequence. This example does so with a V-I cadence.

In the eighteenth-century style, dissonances are always handled with care. They are prepared by common tone ahead of time, turn dissonant as the other voices move, and are resolved downward by step. That's why the "launching note" gets played first in Example 2.9; it's the preparation. (Unprepared and unresolved dissonances will immediately make your improvisation sound twentieth century.)

Even though you could keep it going until you run out of keys on the piano, sequences usually stop at cadences, which we will study more later. When

EXAMPLE 2.9   Descending 7-6 sequence in major and minor.

EXAMPLE 2.10   Descending 7-6 with upper voices traded.

playing sequences in minor, use the natural form of the scale to avoid augmented second leaps. You will notice that it sounds like it's going back into major. If you want to keep it in minor and bring it to a stop, you have to find a place to raise the leading tone and make a cadence, as in measure 10 of Example 2.9.

When you play sequences, the notes form chords (obviously). But you needn't focus too much on what those chords are. You don't have to analyze as you go: "Hmm. This is like an A minor 7, and this is like an F in first inversion, and this one is kind of a G7." That's all true, but you can just follow the sequence pattern and not worry about the analysis. There are other times when we need to pay very careful attention to exactly what chord we are on, but in sequences we pay more attention to the pattern of intervals than the chords.

The upper voices in a 7-6 sequence can trade places. For a variant, let's put the dissonant voice in the middle as shown in the top line of Example 2.10. Notice that the 7-6 intervals are now between the middle and bottom voices.

EXERCISE: Play the 7-6 sequence in a simple three voice texture, using Example 2.9 as a guide. Notice that every voice moves downward by step, just not at the same time. Now try the variant form of the sequence, in which the upper voices trade places (see Example 2.10). When you are comfortable in C, transpose to several other keys, and play both variants. Be sure to try several minor keys as well, staying in the natural form of the scale until you wish to exit the sequence, at which point you must raise the leading tone.

Connecting the Page One Opener and the Descending 7-6 Sequence

In Example 2.11 we see three positions of the Page One (in three voices) connecting to a 7-6 sequence. Depending on the position of the Page One (i.e., which note of the chord is at the top), the sequence will start in different places, with different chords and different bass notes.

When you connect the Page One to the sequence, you can use any note from the I chord as the launching note of the sequence. This is your preparation, which is consonant because it's part of the I chord, but becomes dissonant as the other voices move into place to start the sequence.

EXERCISE: Play the Page One in three-voice block chords and launch a 7-6 sequence. Try this in all positions of the Page One, and in several keys, including minor. Once you start the sequence, carry it on for a while. Find ways to exit the sequence and create a V-I (or V-i) cadence.

There is another way to launch the 7-6 sequence. Instead of using one of the tonic's notes as a launcher, we can raise the tonic chord's fifth to a sixth. It works as shown in Example 2.12.

EXERCISE: Play the Page One and use the "5-6 launcher" to start the 7-6 sequence. Try both variants as shown in Example 2.12. Do this in several keys.

EXAMPLE 2.11   Three positions of the Page One with Descending 7-6.

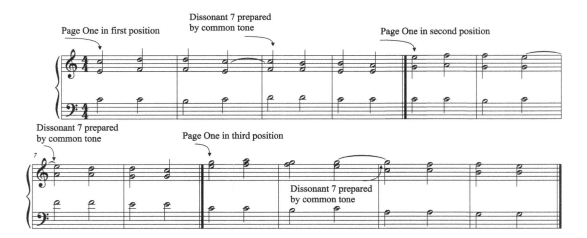

EXAMPLE 2.12   Launching a 7-6 descending sequence by raising the 5th of the chord.

Notice that this does not work well when the Page One is in first position for two reasons: our usual three-voice version of the Page One does not contain the fifth of the tonic triad, and the outer voices will create parallel octaves.

Cadence: ii-V-I

Cadences conclude sections of music and confirm a key area. Cadences take many forms ranging from the simplest V-I progression to complex, multichord events replete with highly active motions in all voices. For now, we will learn a simple ii-V-I progression. The ii chord will normally appear in first inversion (ii^6). Note that in minor keys, the ii chord is diminished (ii^o). When possible, you may use a ii^7 chord, which will be incomplete (missing the fifth) when played in three voices. Of course, you may use an incomplete V^7 as well. Three voices very often require incomplete chords. As long as each chord has (at least) a root and third, all is well. Example 2.13 shows ten possible ii-V-I cadences, five in major and five in minor, starting in various positions. Note that some are triads only, and some include chord sevenths. These are not the only possible ways to play ii-V-I. As a start, though, you should acquire mastery over this cadence in any position (e.g., no matter which chord factor is in the soprano as you start the pattern) and any key. (In the chapter on partimento, we will learn the historic approach to cadences, but for now we will continue to use the contemporary terminology with which you are probably familiar.)

EXERCISE: Learn the ii-V-I cadence thoroughly. You will use this cadence countless times in your improvisation studies, so you may as well learn it in every key now. This investment of time will save you from stumbling around in your improvisations later.

Example 2.14 shows four ways that a 7-6 sequence may connect with a ii-V-I cadence. A simple way is to descend through the sequence until the bass reaches ④, which supports the ii^6 chord. The first two passages in the example show this possibility. In the third passage, the sequence starts with the bass on

EXAMPLE 2.13 ii-V-I cadences.

EXAMPLE 2.14 Connecting 7-6 descending sequences with ii-V-I cadences.

④, which means the sequence would have to descend through a complete octave, seeming disproportionately long. Therefore, it descends to ①, from which it leaps upward to begin the cadence. The fourth instance shows the bass descending past ④, then going back up to it.

Making a list of every way to connect sequences to cadences is impossible. We might as well try to make a list of all possible sentences that describe the weather. However, in language you do not need to know every possible way to say something. You do need at least one; if you want to be an interesting conversationalist, you might want a few more. Music is the same. Do not worry about every possibility; instead, gain mastery over the examples given here, and perhaps discover a few more on your own.

EXERCISE: Practice connecting both variants of the 7-6 descending sequence to different positions of the ii-V-I cadence as shown in the previous examples. Do this in several major and minor keys. Note that your sequences will vary in length depending on how you start and end them.

Combining Three Techniques

Now we have three musical techniques: the Page One opener, the descending 7-6 sequence, and the ii-V-I cadence. Let's put them together.

EXERCISE: Use chords in three voices. Choose a key. Play a Page One, launch a descending 7-6 sequence, and conclude with a ii-V-I cadence. Try the Page One in the three different positions, and note how this affects the length of your 7-6 sequence. Don't forget to try the 5-6 launcher also. Try various ways of connecting with the ii-V-I cadence by tracking the bass line and deciding how to get to ④. Play in time. Go as slowly as you like, but play musically. Do this in every key, and try various time signatures, noting the adjustments you must make for different meters. Keep working at it until you can get all the way through while keeping steady rhythm. The more you repeat this exercise in a wide variety of keys, the stronger your improvisational thinking will become.

Modulations

Music that stays in the same key too long can get boring. Eighteenth-century music changes key frequently and uses these harmonic contrasts as part of the drama. In short pieces like dance suite movements, major pieces usually move to the dominant by the mid-point, and spend the second half of the piece getting back home. Minor pieces often go either to the relative major or minor dominant, and again use the second section to get home again.

Music can modulate to any key. We will start, however, with four modulations that are the most common in this style. From a major key we will modulate to V and vi (and back home again). From a minor key we will modulate to III and v (and back).

Modulation often requires two events which may happen in succession or simultaneously. First, we must alter the scale to match the new key. This is called a *scale mutation*. In doing so, we start to get the sound of the new key. Second, we must confirm the new key with a cadence. Example 2.15 shows these events in succession. Example 2.16 shows them happening at the same time.

EXAMPLE 2.15   Scale mutation within the 7-6 descending sequence.

EXAMPLE 2.16   Scale mutation within the cadence.

EXAMPLE 2.17   Three ways to exit a sequence.

In our improvisations, sequences will connect to modulations. Therefore, we will learn to alter the scale during sequences to start the process of modulation. A note you must alter frequently is the leading tone of the new key. If you are in C major and want to modulate to V, you need the leading tone of G, which is F♯. At some point in your sequence, flip the Fs into F♯s. That will accomplish the first stage of modulation, the scale mutation. (When modulating from a minor key to its relative major, the crucial scale mutation is lowering the minor key's leading tone, e.g., from c minor to E♭ the B♮ must be flatted. However, since sequences in minor use the natural scale, the necessary scale mutation is already done once the sequence gets going.) Next, exit the sequence and play a cadence. Example 2.17 shows three ways to do that. Note that in this example, the sequence exits and goes to the new tonic, which is then confirmed after the fact with a ii-V-I cadence.

Remember to make the final I chord land on a relatively strong beat. You can freely alter the rhythmic values of chords in a cadence in order to make things land on the beats you want.

Modulation to V and vi from major keys, and to v from minor keys, always involves finding the leading tone of the new key and introducing it into the sequence, either prior to or during a cadence. This sounds like a simple principle, but you will need to practice modulating quite a bit in order to become comfortable. Example 2.18 provides guidance.

EXERCISE: Practice starting sequences in major keys and modulating to V or vi. Then start a sequence in the new key and modulate back to your first

EXAMPLE 2.18   Modulating to nearby keys using sequences.

key. Do the same for minor keys moving to III and v and back again. Note that ⑥ in the bass will sometimes need to raise or lower.

Improvising a Complete Piece with Chords

We now know how to play the Page One, the 7-6 descending sequence, a ii-V-I cadence, and some modulations. We are ready to arrange these into a complete piece.

Here is a plan for a piece in a major key:

Page One
Sequence to V or vi
Cadence in V or vi
Page One in V or vi
Sequence to I
Cadence in I

Here is a plan for a piece in a minor key:

Page One
Sequence to III or v
Cadence in III or v
Page One in III or v
Sequence to I
Cadence in I

EXERCISE: Play these plans as chords in three voices in lots of keys. Before you begin, review the key areas you will visit. What are the key signatures and leading tones? Play slowly and patiently; at first, you will find it very challenging to keep everything straight in your head. As soon as you can do it in one key,

EXAMPLE 2.19 Block chords solutions for the improvisation plan.

change to another. Because you are using two descending sequences, your piece may end up too low on the piano. A good place to jump to a higher octave is immediately after a cadence.

Example 2.19 presents four possible solutions for the two plans. These solutions illustrate the use of the second and third positions of the Page One. You should also note a variety of rhythmic durations of cadences, placement of scale mutations, uses of sequence variants, and ways of getting into and out of sequences. Go through the solutions and identify each of our improvisational techniques; I've deliberately not labeled them to leave you a challenge.

Figuration

Now that we understand how to assemble various chordal techniques into short pieces, at last it is time to add figuration so that our improvisations will sound like real music from the eighteenth century. In its simplest form figuration is merely breaking up chords into consistent, individual note patterns, as in the C major prelude from WTC I, the source of the Page One progression.

EXAMPLE 2.20   The Umpadeeda figuration.

Since we have been working in three-voice chords, we will start with a three-voice texture as we add figuration. An example of this technique is the Prelude in B♭ from WTC I. The first half of the piece consists entirely of three-voice chords broken into consistent figuration. This pattern—a note in the bass followed by middle, top, and middle notes in the right hand—is very common. I would venture to say that it is the most frequent pattern applied to three-voice textures. I call it the *umpadeeda* because that is how you pronounce the rhythm. See Example 2.20.

EXERCISE: Apply the umpadeeda to the various techniques we have studied thus far. Start with the Page One, and then apply figuration to both variants of the 7-6 descending sequence and several versions of the ii-V-I cadence. When each of these techniques seems under control, put them together. Work your way up to playing complete figuration preludes using the two plans from the previous section, which include modulations. Example 2.21 shows figuration applied to the first two progressions from Example 2.19. The umpadeeda may be transformed into a triplet rhythm by dropping the last note. If you wish, you can practice adding figuration to chords by keeping Example 2.19 in front of you.

A New Opener: Quiescenza

Page One isn't the only opener in town. Here is another in Example 2.22.

Robert Gjerdingen named the *Quiescenza* (the term means "rest") because it often appears after important cadences and serves to dissipate the energy of the concluded section of music. However, the same pattern may also serve as an opener, in which function its character is more likely to be declamatory and dramatic. While Gjerdingen describes the pattern in terms of outer voices only, for our purposes we will consider it as a progression of three-voice chords. The Quiescenza starts on the I chord, lowers ❼ to make a secondary dominant, moves to IV, then V (or vii°) and returns to I again. Importantly, this must all

EXAMPLE 2.21 Figuration applied to chord progressions.

EXAMPLE 2.22 Quiescenza.

happen over a tonic pedal point. In eighteenth-century music the Quiescenza is as common as the Page One.

You can use the Quiescenza in the same way as the Page One: as an opener or as a middle section after a sequence. It works equally well in major or minor.

EXERCISE: Practice the Quiescenza in all the same ways you practiced Page One.

Sequence: 5-6 Ascending

The 7-6 sequence descends. We should learn a sequence that ascends, as well. The 5-6 ascending sequence appears in Example 2.23.

EXAMPLE 2.23   Ascending 5-6 sequence.

As with the 7-6, we see it in two variants. The 5-6 ascending sequence launches from a root position triad. Just like 7-6 descending, it can go as far as you like. As with all sequences, minor versions use the natural form of the scale until we want to leave the sequence, at which point we introduce the raised leading tone. However, when exiting the sequence we must avoid the interval of the augmented second, so the 5-6 will use the melodic form of the minor scale if the bass ascends ⑥-⑦-①.

The 5-6 sequence starts with a triad in root position. The fifth of the chord steps up to a sixth, followed by the other two voices in parallel motion. The second variant shown in the example reverses the position of the top two voices; this is exactly the same way the 7-6 descending sequences gets its other variant.

EXERCISE: Choose a key. Start on the tonic triad and launch a 5-6 ascending sequence. Connect it to a cadence. Try a minor 5-6 as well, and exit by adding the leading tone and playing a cadence.

A New Ending: The Quiescenza (Again)

The Quiescenza may serve as an ending as well as an opener. We have already explained its harmonic structure. A variant skips the penultimate dominant harmony, and thus contains one harmonic event fewer than the typical Quiescenza. Example 2.24 shows a Quiescenza without dominant harmony.

EXERCISE: Learn this pattern in many different keys, first with block chords and then with figurations. Return to the improvisation plans presented previously, and replace the final ii-V-I cadences with Quiescenzas, or keep the ii-V-I and add a Quiescenza (either variant) after it.

We will learn another ending in addition to the Quiescenza.

EXAMPLE 2.24   Quiescenza without dominant harmony.

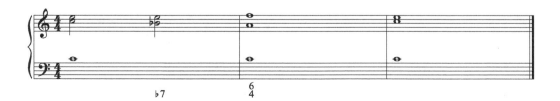

Converging Cadence

Example 2.25 shows the converging cadence, which approaches the final I by means of the ii or IV chord. The bass then climbs chromatically, creating a secondary dominant of V. V^7 is suspended. V^7 then resolves to a suspended I, which in turn resolves. This progression derives drama from the secondary dominant and the suspended chords.

EXERCISE: Learn the converging cadence in several keys, first as block chords and then with figuration. On your own, figure out how it works in a minor key. Return to the improvisation plans presented previously, and replace the ii-V-I cadences with converging cadences. If you want to sound extra epic, try a converging cadence followed by a Quiescenza.

Using All the Techniques Together

Now we are ready to improvise figuration preludes using all the techniques at once. Spend a great deal of time on this over several days. This level of improvisation is already quite sophisticated and makes significant demands on your mental powers. Be patient and persistent.

EXERCISE: Choose a key and time signature. Play each of the following plans, first with three-voice block chords and then with figuration. Make up your own plans, as well.

Plan #1 (Major Key):

Page One in I
Desc 7-6 to V
Cadence in V
Page One in V
Asc 5-6 to vi
Cadence in vi
Page One in vi
Desc 7-6 to I
Cadence in I
Quiescenza in I

EXAMPLE 2.25 Converging cadence.

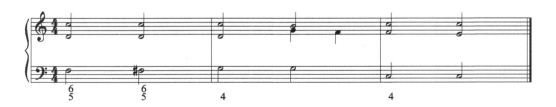

Plan #2 (Major Key):

Quiescenza in I
Asc 5-6 to vi
Cadence in vi
Page One in vi
Desc 7-6 to V
Cadence in V
Quiescenza in V
Asc 5-6 to I
Converging Cadence in I

Plan #3 (Minor Key):

Page One in i
Asc 5-6 to III
Quiescenza in III
Desc 7-6 to v
Page One in v
Asc 5-6 to i
Quiescenza in i

Plan #4 (Minor Key):

Quiescenza in i
Desc 7-6 to v
Cadence in v
Page One in v
Asc 5-6 to III
Cadence in III
Quiescenza in III
Desc 7-6 to i
Converging Cadence in i
Quiescenza in i

A possible solution for Plan #1 appears in Example 2.26.

Additional Figuration

Our initial foray into figuration was limited to three voices with chord tones only. We will now expand our vocabulary by considering further levels of complexity in figuration texture.

We have already studied the simplest possible texture: three voices, using chord tones only. You should now be able to break up three-voice chords into figuration without much trouble. The limitation of this approach is the sparse variety of patterns that you can create with three voices and chord tones only.

EXAMPLE 2.26   Solution to Plan #1.

As we expand our vocabulary of figurations we can begin allowing for simultaneously sounding notes and doublings at the octave (especially the bass). This approach has the advantages of allowing for a richer sound at the piano and more interesting patterns, while still leaving the harmonic progression fairly clear and manageable. One way to double the bass is to jump up and down by an octave, a very common technique.

Advancing to further complexity, we can add passing tones. This approach significantly enriches the sound of a three voice-voice texture and introduces a more melodic sound, since the neighbor and passing tones allow for stepwise motion within the figuration. Most commonly, the neighbor tones decorate the top or middle voice, although the bass is possible as well.

After mastering three-voice textures, we may try four or more voices with chord tones only. This approach allows for greater harmonic fullness such as complete chords with sevenths. At the same time, voice-leading may become more crowded and unruly.

The final level is four or more voices (or changing the number of voices at will) with neighbor and passing tones, and doubling at the octave if desired. This approach allows for maximum harmonic fullness, including interesting

EXAMPLE 2.27 Examples of figuration.

EXAMPLE 2.28 Further examples of figuration.

sounds such as chords with sevenths and even ninths. It is also possible to create a more Romantic piano sound using this technique; Busoni frequently used it in his Bach transcriptions. Managing the voice-leading and nonharmonic tones can become very challenging. Once we start to add neighbor and passing notes, it becomes less clear how many voices we are implying. At this stage, as long as the voice-leading sounds good and the harmony is correct, it is not important to keep strict accounting of the number of voices.

Example 2.27 shows a series of figurations. Each is based on the Page One progression except the last which is an excerpt from J. C. F. Fischer's "Clio" suite, showing a four-voice figuration with a suspension.

Example 2.28 shows additional figuration examples from various composers. Check them out and find interesting figurations to borrow, customize, and steal for your own. All these compositions, in whole or in part, use figuration to elaborate upon underlying chord progressions. Naturally, you will now be curious to study a variety of composers to learn about their characteristic figurations.

EXERCISE: Go back to your improvisation plans from the previous exercise. Select or invent figurations, and practice various plans in many different keys. Keep your figurations rhythmically even, patterned consistently, and as expressive as you can. You should work with a metronome to develop rhythmic discipline. When you are comfortable with the process, improvise a figuration prelude for your friends, or record yourself and critique the results. Finally, develop a personal collection of figurations in various meters and keys and copy them into your zibaldone.

Chapter 3

Toccata

The word toccata means "touch," a reference to hands touching a keyboard. In other words, a toccata is a piece that showcases idiomatic keyboard playing. While I have chosen for convenience to use the term "toccata," this same style of playing could just as easily be called fantasia or prelude.

In order to learn to improvise in the toccata style, we will survey a variety of compositions, note what musical and stylistic elements they employ, and create our own collection of toccata building-blocks. We will then assemble those blocks into satisfying, stylistically coherent pieces.

Toccatas may be measured or unmeasured. That is, they may exist in a specific meter with precise rhythmic notation, or they may be rhythmically free. An unmeasured piece may still have bar lines, but the number of beats does not necessarily add up, and the listener may not always hear a clear beat. In unmeasured music the smallest rhythmic divisions (whether the fastest notes are in sixteenths or triplets, for example) are usually consistent within each phrase, so that each gesture of the improvisation may seem to have its own internal sense of pulse. Another way to think of unmeasured music is to imagine that each phrase is more or less in rhythm, but the phrases may be separated by pauses or fermatas. The unmeasured style requires the performer to provide sensible rhythmic pacing and rhetorical delivery such that each moment of the music sounds as if it is on the way toward or arriving at an important event.

The toccata need not have a main theme. In contrast with the fugue, which is built upon an oft-repeated subject, the toccata may not have any unifying thematic material. Indeed, it may proceed as a musical stream of consciousness as far as themes are concerned.

Patterned Elaboration (PE) and Whole Note Chords (WNC)

We will now begin assembling a collection of toccata building blocks. Giuseppe Sarti (1729–1802) will provide the first two, which we observe in his Preludio from the sonata in G for Harpsichord. See Example 3.1. This composition consists of nothing but two building blocks: a figuration applied to various harmonies, and whole note chords (intended to be arpeggiated freely in performance).

The first building block is an obvious strategy to decorate and extend a harmony, and to do so in a way that uses much of the keyboard's range, which is appropriate for the toccata style. You could easily substitute almost any figuration for Sarti's, and the composition would not change very much. Through

EXAMPLE 3.1   Giuseppe Sarti's Prelude in G.

most of the piece, the pattern elaborates one harmony at a time (although from measure 9 to measure 10, a chord change occurs). We will call this building block *Patterned Elaboration* (PE).

The second building block, chords written as long notes but played as arpeggios, appears very frequently in eighteenth-century keyboard music. The normal way to realize them is to arpeggiate the written notes from bottom to top and back down again, then a second time if desired. Some performers will even sweep through them three times, or apply a more complex pattern to the entire chord. (Modern harpsichord players retain this tradition; listen to their recordings if you need a clearer idea.) The function of the chords in this piece is to move the music forward to new harmonic territory. We will call this building block *Whole Note Chords* (WNC), even though in some pieces the same idea may appear in other rhythmic values such as half notes.

Unlike many other eighteenth-century keyboard textures, WNC allows unlimited doublings of parts, as well as some parallel motion in the inner voices. (Some parallels cannot be heard when hidden in the middle of a dense keyboard texture.) The outer voices, however, must avoid parallel fifths and octaves.

Here is the overall plan of Sarti's piece:

PE presents a G major chord (I)
Whole Note Chords (WNC) moves the harmony to A minor (ii)
PE presents A minor (ii) and F♯ diminished chords (vii°)
WNC moves the harmony toward the vicinity of D minor (v)
PE presents a C♯ diminished chord (vii°/v)
WNC moves the harmony back to G major (I)
PE confirms G major (I)

EXERCISE: We can use Sarti's two building blocks to improvise our own short toccatas. First, play Sarti's original. Then try the toccata plans that follow. In the WNC sections, you will need to select the appropriate chords to move to the target harmony (you may need to work this out in advance). You can use as many or few chords as you like. For the PE you can use Sarti's or invent one of you own. A possible solution for each plan appears in Example 3.2.

Plan for Major Key Toccata

PE in I
WNC moves the harmony to V
PE in V
WNC moves the harmony to vi
PE in vi
WNC moves the harmony to I
PE in I

EXAMPLE 3.2.1 AND 3.2.2 Major and minor solutions for the Sarti improvisation plan.

EXAMPLE 3.2.1 AND 3.2.2   Continued

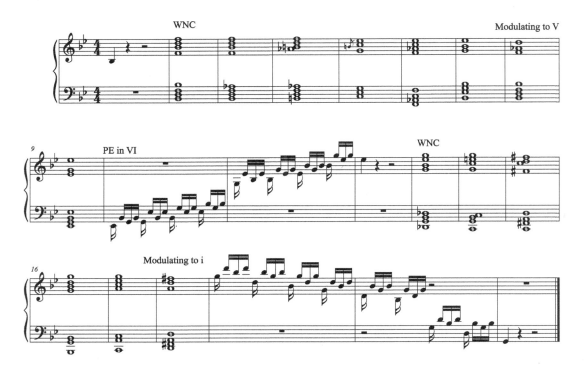

Plan for a Minor Key Toccata

PE in i
WNC moves the harmony to III
PE in III
WNC moves the harmony to VI
PE in VI
WNC moves the harmony to i
PE in i

In this exercise we used PE to extend a single harmony into a longer, more interesting musical event. We will now explore a wider variety of PE strategies, discover how to use them to get lots of mileage out of a single chord, and add them to our collection of improvisatory building blocks.

The first six measures of Example 3.3 show a figured bass as it appears in a toccata by Alessandro Scarlatti (1660–1725). The next six measures show one possible solution in block chords with some doublings of voices. In the 1922 Ricordi edition of Scarlatti's works, editor Alessandro Longo provided fully realized "performance interpretations" for this same bass line, two measures of which appear at the end of Example 3.3. Essentially, Longo fills in the harmonies indicated by the figured bass, then notates them as written-out WNCs. (While intended to help modern pianists know what to play, Longo's practice also serves as evidence of the abandonment of even simple improvisational skills from the classical performance tradition in the twentieth century.)

EXAMPLE 3.3 Alessandro Scarlati's toccata.

We will take these six measures in a different direction. Instead of playing them as WNCs, we will realize them with PEs.

EXERCISE: Realize Scarlatti's bass with block chords, using good voice-leading for the outer parts. Note the suspensions indicated by the figured bass. Make sure you understand the harmonic analysis, and transpose the progression into other minor keys. Learn it as thoroughly as you learned the Page One.

Example 3.4 shows many ways to apply PE to a C major chord. Some are limited to chord tones while others use neighbor and passing tones, or an entire scale. Example 3.4 is by no means a complete list of possibilities. You can find endless examples in eighteenth-century music, and you can invent your own. (Although whatever you come up with, someone has probably already used it. There is nothing new under the sun.) PEs must emphasize chord tones often enough that the sound of the chord comes through; if the PE sounds like a random sampling of the whole scale, it's wrong.

EXERCISE: Using the PEs from Example 3.4 and your own ideas, practice navigating around the keyboard with the right hand, outlining Scarlatti's progression. The left hand can play bass notes only, on the downbeat. Go slowly, in rhythm, and get to know each pattern thoroughly, in several different keys.

EXERCISE: Now we will take the PE material we just learned and turn it upside down. This time the right hand will play the chords of the Scarlatti progression on the downbeat while the left hand extends each harmony with PEs. The patterns we just learned for the right hand will work in the left also. Finally, figure out how to make a major key version of this same

EXAMPLE 3.4 Patterned Elaborations on a C major chord.

progression. Example 3.5 shows three possible solutions for the "upside down" version.

One of the great challenges of improvisation is knowing where to go harmonically. A short progression like Scarlatti's runs out quickly. This can stop us in our tracks. Jazz musicians improvising on standard tunes never have this problem because they simply loop through the underlying progression over and over. An improvisation over the relatively short 12-bar blues pattern may involve dozens of repetitions of the same chord progression. Classical improvisers, then, should not hesitate to get a little more mileage out of individual chords.

EXERCISE: Go back through the previous exercise. Choose some of the PEs from Example 3.4 and extend them to several measures by using the

EXAMPLE 3.5   "Upside-down" version of Scarlatti's chords.

alternating hands approach: after elaborating each chord with PEs in the right hand, continue the same chord by placing PEs in the left hand. Additionally, explore the literature of eighteenth-century composers you love, find ideas for extending harmonies through interesting patterns, steal them, and write them in your zibaldone. As always, practice them in many different keys, then try to extend each chord of the Scarlatti progression into a fairly long event. By the time you are done extending all six chords, you will have created a surprisingly

EXAMPLE 3.6 Patterned Elaborations on Scarlatti's chords.

substantial piece of music. Example 3.6 provides three illustrations of PEs applied to the first two measures of the Scarlatti progression (but doubled to last four measures). The complete version in Example 3.7 may appear rather ambitious, but it consists of nothing but the Scarlatti chords and PEs in the form of scales.

Of course, the Scarlatti bass ends on V, so it doesn't work as a complete piece (the original served as a prelude to a subsequent composition). To extend it into a longer work, we will now learn the next building block.

The Circle of Fifths (C5)

Even though we can now wring quite a bit of music from a few chords, we still want to venture to new harmonic territory. An excellent way to visit every harmony within a single key is to use a *Circle of Fifths* progression, or C5 for short. This harmonic pattern is ubiquitous in Western music and shows up in everything from Vivaldi's *Seasons* to *Autumn Leaves*. Knowing the C5 is indispensable for the improviser.

The C5 at its most basic level is a series of chords with bass notes a fifth apart from each other. The bass line moves by falling fifths. The most important harmonic move in all Western music is the V–I progression. The V–I is the wind-up spring of the Happy Meal toy of music: it makes it go. The circle takes that same intervallic relationship of the falling fifth and maps it across every possible location within the key. (Note that when C5s are contained within a key signature, one of the fifth leaps will be diminished: in major,

EXAMPLE 3.7.1 AND 3.7.2 Ambitious Patterned Elaboration on Scarlatti's chords.

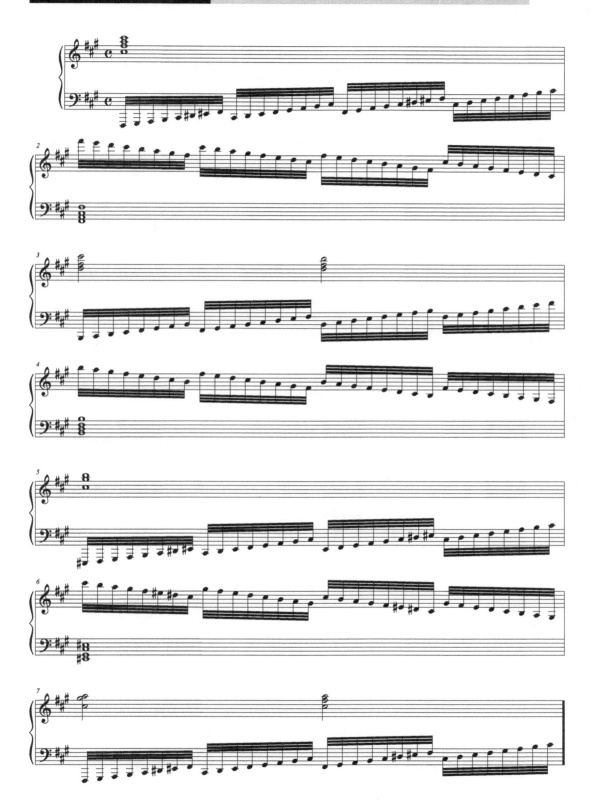

EXAMPLE 3.7.1 AND 3.7.2   Continued

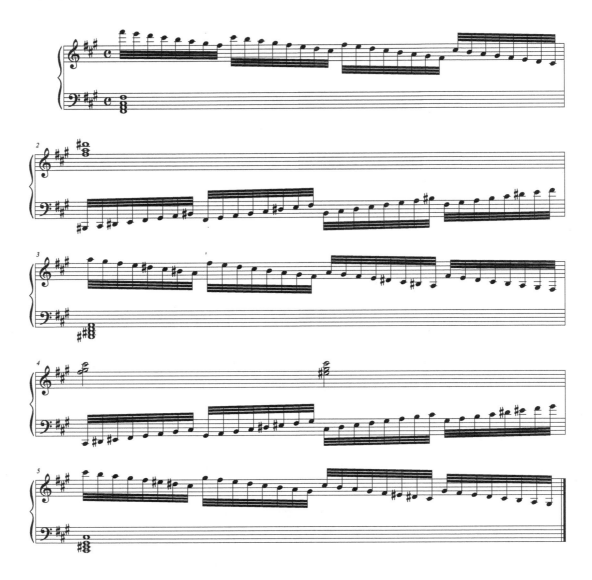

between ④ and ⑦, and in minor between ⑥ and ②. If you keep all the fifths perfect, you will move from one key to another until you have navigated all the way around the harmonic world.)

Even though the bass theoretically moves in falling fifths, we don't actually play it that way because the line would drop off the left end of the piano. Falling fifths appear in real music as alternating falling fifths and rising fourths, which keeps them in a reasonable range.

When playing C5s in major keys, simply stay within the key signature. In minor keys, use the natural form of the scale until you reach the V chord, at which point you must raise ❼. (You may recall that this is the way we handled the minor scale in sequences when we studied figuration preludes.)

Voice-leading considerations tend to make the upper voices move by step, small leap, and common tone. This balances the large leaps in the bass.

C5s may appear in many guises. One form is triads. A higher level of complexity is to make some or all of the triads into seventh chords. This results in very satisfying voice-leading as the third of each chord becomes the seventh of the next chord by common tone. All these versions of the C5 appear in Example 3.8. The third version shows how eighteenth century masters taught this pattern: two upper voices moving by step, and always including the seventh above the bass. Many other guises of circle progressions are possible, but we will begin with the ones just mentioned.

You will need to take some time at the piano to gain familiarity with circle progressions. Trained classical pianists know their scales and arpeggios very well (or ought to!) but are often surprised at their own unfamiliarity with other ways of traversing a key. Playing scales and arpeggios is like visiting a town every day by driving through on Main Street. There are neighborhoods and parks you never see if you only take Main Street.

EXERCISE: In order to familiarize yourself with the C5, play Example 3.8 first as block chords in many keys, and then improvise figuration preludes on them. Do so in duple and compound meters. (A circle progression, all by itself, makes for a perfectly adequate figuration prelude.) Note that the example contains settings in three and four voices.

EXERCISE: Once you have gained familiarity with C5s, apply PEs to them. Choose one PE that you know very well and use it on each chord of a C5. Start by playing the bass as a strong note on the downbeat. Then do your PE up and down the keyboard. Then play the next bass note followed by the appropriate PE, and so on. If you're unsure how to start, uses Sarti's PE. Do this in several major and minor keys. Example 3.9 shows two solutions.

EXAMPLE 3.8 C5 progressions.

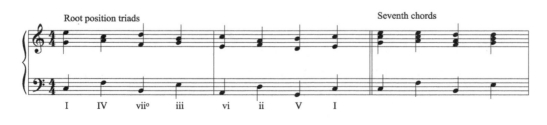

EXAMPLE 3.9   C5 with Patterned Elaborations.

EXERCISE: Let us now create short toccatas by connecting the Scarlatti chords with a C5. The C5 will provide the V-I cadence that was missing in Scarlatti, so the improvisation will sound more complete. As a starting point, play only bass notes (or octaves if you prefer) in the left hand, and do all the PEs in the right hand, using patterns such as those in Example 3.4, or creating your own. As you become more confident, give the left hand more active material in your improvisation. Try this exercise in several major and minor keys. Example 3.10 shows a possible solution. Example 3.11, a more complex realization, includes a C5 with suspensions as well as some other interesting dissonances.

The Scarlatti bass combined with the C5, overlayed with PEs, opens nearly infinite pathways of improvisation. For example, you could play the whole

EXAMPLE 3.10   Root position C5 with Patterned Elaborations.

structure (Scarlatti + C5) once using WNCs, then repeat using more active, up-tempo PEs. Before continuing with this chapter, continue working on the material presented thus far until you can fluently improvise several versions in a variety of major and minor keys, using PE, WNC, and C5.

Building Blocks from Bach

Bach's Chromatic Fantasy, BWV 903, can contribute to our understanding of the toccata style. Its opening presents four of the composer's building blocks in quick succession. We already know one of them, so we will steal the other three. Example 3.12 shows the first four building blocks of the Chromatic Fantasy.

EXAMPLE 3.11   C5 with suspensions.

The opening statement is simply a pair of flourishes made mostly of scales outlining i-V and then answering with V-i. Note that the highest and lowest notes of the flourishes provide good voice-leading. Next comes a passage defined by parallel tenths in the outer voices, with a static middle voice. Arriving at V, that chord is elaborated briefly with an arpeggio. A second such passage follows with the upper notes in a different order, and another elaboration of V via arpeggio. Next, we encounter a C5 in quick harmonic rhythm, expressed in sparse arpeggiated figures of alternating close and open spacing. The final element is the descending fauxbourdon passage, which is comprised of parallel first-inversion triads (or chords of the sixth). Fauxbourdon is a very old technique, dating back to the dawn of harmony. It is the only permissible way to write parallel stepwise chords—until Debussy.

EXAMPLE 3.12   The first four building blocks of the Bach's Chromatic Fantasy.

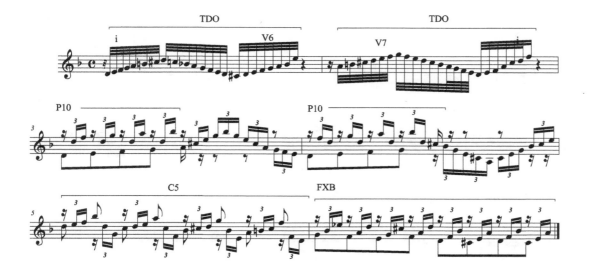

EXAMPLE 3.13   Tonic-Dominant Oscillations.

Though these events are impressive and even bewildering when played in quick succession, with some study we can realize their underlying simplicity and appropriate them for our collection of toccata building blocks.

EXERCISE: Start with the i-V and V-i flourishes in the first two measures. For short, let's call this building block the *Tonic-Dominant Oscillation*, or TDO. Invent several of your own TDOs that use these same harmonies. Make sure the bottom and top notes of your passages outline sensible voice-leading. Use scales only, arpeggios only, and then a mix of the two. Of course, try it in several keys including major. Example 3.13 shows three instances of two-voice outlines realized into full TDOs.

EXERCISE: Next, we will appropriate the tenths section. We'll call this building block *Parallel Tenths* (P10). Begin on ① in the bass and go up to ⑤ by

EXAMPLE 3.14 Parallel 10ths (P10).

step. One of the upper voices must stay in parallel tenths with the bass while the other voice is unmoved on ❶. Invent several versions of this gesture and play them in many keys including major. Example 3.14 shows instances of P10. Of course, P10 is not limited to bass lines that walk from ① to ⑤. It can be used in a wide variety of harmonic situations. For now, however, make sure you are confident with this first step.

EXERCISE: We already know about the C5. However, Bach's version is particularly clever; even though it is a simple traversal of all the chords within the home key, its audacious voicing trades between cramped stepwise and expansive open spacings, almost as if the chords are compressed and then exploded. Learn this exact voicing of the progression. Then invent your own, as well. As always, transpose. Create versions that take more time and use more notes for each chord, as shown in Example 3.15.

EXERCISE: Let's call the fauxbourdon building block the FXB. The FXB is very flexible. Built entirely of parallel first-inversion triads, it can move consistently in one direction, or zig-zig as Bach does. It may ascend or descend, although the latter is more common. It can go for a short distance or quite far, and cadence in the home key or modulate. FXB passages can go as far as you want, but of course must stop before sounding ridiculous. If you intend to descend a long way in minor, you should use the natural form of the scale until you approach a V chord. Start by trying FXB passages in simple block chords. Then apply various figurations to them, like a figuration prelude. Example 3.16 provides some guidance.

EXAMPLE 3.15   C5 progressions.

EXAMPLE 3.16   Fauxbourdon examples.

EXERCISE: After you have worked on all these building blocks, improvise short pieces in various keys using the four building blocks from the Chromatic Fantasy according to the following plans. Fortunately, the dramatic pauses inherent in this style make it easier to put the blocks together. You can also make

EXAMPLE 3.17 Major solution for Chromatic Fantasy improvisation plan.

up your own plans. Example 3.17 provides a solution for the major key plan, and Example 3.18 does so for the minor.

Major Key Plan

TDO
C5
P10
FXB
Conclude with a ii-V-I cadence

EXAMPLE 3.18 Minor solution for Chromatic Fantasy improvisation plan.

Minor Key Plan

C5
TDO
FXB
P10 (in relative major)
Conclude with a V-i cadence

Toccata in D minor, BWV 565

We must not overlook the most famous toccata of all: BWV 565, normally attributed to Bach, shown in Example 3.19. Just like the other examples in this chapter, it is made of building blocks that we may study and appropriate. Even though it appears in the score as a measured composition, the pauses between events and the diverse rhythmic configurations convey some of the qualities of an unmeasured piece. We will go through the entire piece to discover its building blocks. Some of them will turn out to be familiar.

Tonic-Dominant Oscillation (TDO)

The opening employs repeated rhetorical gestures outlining the tonic harmony. It is possible to argue that an implied V chord is included due to the presence of the leading tone. This means that we have encountered something similar to the TDO, a building block we know already. In this instance, the bold musical gestures interspersed with dramatic pauses make for effective rhetoric, despite the sparse harmonic movement.

While the harmonic moves are very simple, their rhetorical organization may be what gives them communicative power. This is a promising thought because improvisers sometimes feel at a loss if we run out of chords to use. But if we practice staying within a limited harmonic zone while developing compelling rhetorical structures, we will find our improvisations greatly enriched.

Patterned Elaboration (PE)

The next passage demonstrates a way to extend single harmonies over long periods and compensate for the static harmony by providing a moving line with energetic rhythmic divisions. The long triplet lines, upon closer inspection, are really just the root, third, and fifth of the tonic triad, surrounded by neighboring tones. The two phrases are identical, of course, except for the octave transposition.

EXERCISE: Study the passage in question, and learn to outline major and minor triads in the same manner, practicing in several different keys. While you have already learned some PEs, take this opportunity to expand your vocabulary. Example 3.20 gives you some more ideas.

The Hidden Sequence (HS)

The next passage descends in triplet rhythm and may appear at first glance to be very similar to the one we just studied. There is a crucial difference. Whereas the previous passage merely outlined a single chord, the descending passage is actually a sequence. It is not a series of parallel triads, even though it looks that

EXAMPLE 3.19.1, 3.19.2, 3.19.3   The toccata in D minor, BWV 565.

EXAMPLE 3.19.1, 3.19.2, 3.19.3   Continued

Continued

EXAMPLE 3.20   Outlining triads with Patterned Elaborations.

Buxtehude: Organ Prelude

Alessandro Scarlatti: Keyboard Toccata

Left hand repeats
everything right
hand just did...

way in print. Example 3.21 shows precisely how it works, and gives further ideas for developing your own versions. The examples in 3.21 can be played in one hand alone or doubled at the octave. When inverted, the HS turns out to be our old friend the Descending 7-6. But now instead of a seventh resolving to a sixth, we have a second resolving to a third.

We can take this passage for our building block collection. Let's name it the Hidden Sequence (HS). Like all sequences, it can function to set up a modulation or it can merely traverse a single key area and conclude with a cadence. We learned earlier that sequences in minor usually take the natural form of the scale until they exit the pattern by cadence. This is exactly what we observe here.

EXAMPLE 3.21   The Hidden Sequence.

EXERCISE: Practice this sequence first as block chords in various keys. End each sequence by finding your way to a cadence, either in your starting key, or as a modulation to a new key. Practice starting in a given key, using the sequence, and discovering modulations to related keys such as relative major or minor, dominant, and subdominant. Refer to Example 3.21 for guidance.

The Alternating Pedal Point (APP)

The next event is really wonderful because it sounds great and is easy to study, understand, and steal for our own purposes. We will call it the Alternating Pedal Point (APP). The composer has created a moving line alternating with a pedal tone, but the pedal tone is high enough that the moving line can go above and beneath it. The pedal tone is ❺. (In the eighteenth century any scale degree except ❶ or ❺ for a pedal tone would be unusual.) You can get away with almost any consonances or dissonances against a pedal point. The requirement, though, is that the moving line must have some kind of rhetoric or logic; it can't be just a bunch of random pitches jumping around. We note that the initial gesture is to move upward in one pattern, then change to a new pattern when descending. Example 3.22 shows some ideas for using the APP.

EXERCISE: Try making up your own APPs in major and minor keys. You may use ❶ or ❺ as the pedal tone. Stay in rhythm and find some kind of sensible pattern for the moving voice. What would you do if you had to improvise something like this in a compound meter?

EXAMPLE 3.22   The Alternating Pedal Point.

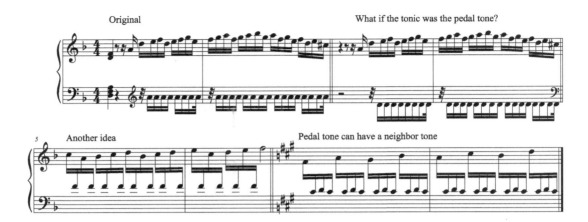

More Fauxbourdon (FXB)

Next, we encounter four repeated FXB approaches to the dominant. The composer gets away with using similar material four times in a row due to variation in the range and rhythmic construction of the passage. (Again, great rhetoric allows limited harmonic ideas to last longer.) A short cadenza follows, consisting of a single line outlining i and V, followed by the FXB approach to the dominant three more times. Before we go on, let us do an exercise.

EXERCISE: Practice APPs connected with a FXB approach to V. Improvise new versions of these passages in several major and minor keys. Example 3.23 provides one idea.

The Long Diminished Chord (LDC)

When we left off our analysis, we had just arrived on V^7. Through a short cadenza passage, that harmony is slightly shifted (by only one note moving a half step) to the leading tone diminished seventh chord. And here we see perhaps the boldest of all harmonic extensions: five full measures of the same chord. Why does it work? The answer again is rhetoric. Imagine if the music held a single chord for a five-measure fermata, or played the same chord over and over in eighth notes. That would be unbearable. This passage works because on the micro level it expresses the harmony in pleasingly undulating triplets. On the macro level it is one huge phrase that descends and then ascends. Even though it is harmonically static, it is rhetorically very active.

Eighteenth-century composers sometimes employ a Long Diminished Chord (LDC) near the end of a piece, much like a cadenza from a nineteenth-century concerto. Since a diminished seventh harmony could resolve in several different directions, its sound is equivocal, as though it is harmonically lost. That is why it works well to create a passage of dramatic instability. Example 3.24 provides several ideas.

EXAMPLE 3.23   Solution for APP exercise.

EXAMPLE 3.24   The Long Diminished Chord.

EXERCISE: Pianistically speaking, only three diminished seventh chords exist, but they may appear in endlessly diverse patterns. Using Example 3.24 as a reference, develop your own LDC ideas. Be sure to use all three possible diminished seventh chords.

EXERCISE: Review all the building blocks from this piece: Tonic-Dominant Oscillation (TDO), Patterned Elaboration (PE), Hidden Sequence (HS), Alternating Pedal Point (APP), and Long Diminished Chord (LDC). Then improvise short toccatas using the following plans. Examples 3.25 and 3.26 provide a solution for each plan.

TDO

PE

HS (and modulate to V or v)

APP (in V or v)

LDC (use it to find your way back to I or i)

ii-V-I (or ii°-V-i) Cadence

EXAMPLE 3.25.1 AND 3.25.2   Solution for first improvisation plan.

EXAMPLE 3.25.1 AND 3.25.2 Continued

APP

HS (and modulate to vi or III)

PE (in vi or III)

LDC (use it to find your way back to I or i)

ii-V-I (or ii°-V-i) Cadence

TDO

The Bach Toccatas

As mentioned earlier, the word toccata does not have a precise technical meaning beyond its reference to idiomatic keyboard writing. The seven toccatas of J. S. Bach (BWV 910–916) contain fugues, arias, imitative counterpoint, and even chorale-style music. They all begin, however, with writing that we can consider toccata-like: impressive displays of keyboard virtuosity assembled from building blocks that seem improvisatory. We will briefly study each of these openings and consider one of them in greater depth.

EXAMPLE 3.26.1 AND 3.26.2   Solution for second improvisation plan.

EXAMPLE 3.26.1 AND 3.26.2   Continued

F♯ minor, BWV 910

The F♯ minor toccata's opening is shown in Example 3.27. It commences with a Quiescenza. Mixed scales and arpeggios delineate each chord. Chords may seem to be hidden within a scale; after all, if we play all seven notes of the scale, how can we tell which three of them are to be heard as the chord of the moment, and which four are passing tones? Bach tends to place chord tones on strong beats within the scale, and is careful that the beginning note of each passage should tell the listener something important about the harmony. In the first measure of this toccata he also attaches a quick arpeggio to the end of each scale passage, which further clarifies the harmony.

In the second measure, the prominent use of E♮ and A♯ indicate a move to the subdominant chord. The third measure provides the dominant harmony and concluding tonic. Then follows a long tonic pedal point with several chord changes in the right hand, none of which leave the home key. Then comes a surprise move to a secondary dominant, which signals a transition to the next section.

EXAMPLE 3.27   Bach's toccata in F# minor, BWV 910.

From the opening of the F# minor toccata we may make some observations useful to our development as improvisers:

1. A single line in one hand can imply a full chord progression along with melodic interest and rhythmic energy.
2. In such passages, chord tones must appear on strong beats if the harmony is to be clear.
3. It is more interesting to change directions and patterns than to do one thing all the way up or down the keyboard. A comparison of Bach's complex passage with Sarti's PE passages will clarify this point.

C minor, BWV 911

Like the F# minor, the C minor toccata opens with a single line as shown in Example 3.28, eventually supplemented with a pedal point. The implied harmonies are tonic and dominant until the middle of the third measure. At that point a rising series of sixths begins, marked by a loping rhythm and a curious accented lower neighboring tone. Soon a pedal point begins, over which a Quiescenza progression leads to the fermata. Observations:

1. The thirty-second note pairs, appearing first in measure two as double neighbors, become a unifying idea throughout the movement.

EXAMPLE 3.28   Bach's toccata in C minor, BWV 911.

2. The rising sixths in measure three are a flexible improvisational element; like sequences, moving sixths and thirds can travel as long as you like until you wish to break the pattern.

3. Once again chord tones land on strong beats. In this piece, the strong beats are even more emphatic as they also happen to be longer notes, with the quick 32nds "running up" to them.

D major, BWV 912

The D major toccata, shown in Example 3.29, serves as further proof that with sufficient audacity, the performer can extend a single harmony for a very long time. The opening tonic chord takes a full seven measures. However, uneventful harmony must be paid for; in this piece compensation comes in the form of an ascending scale that unfolds into a chord with neighbor tones. It sounds like a firework launched into the air and exploding. The same pattern repeats in descending motion through various voicings of the chord. As if to confirm the bold optimism of these gestures, the first harmonic change is a bracing jump to the secondary dominant, confirmed with a tremolo. The cadence on A major seems understated in comparison. Observations:

1. Extension of a single harmony is the improviser's best friend.

2. Simple transformations of the same material, such as re-voicings of chords or octave transpositions, allow repetition without boredom.

3. The tremolo, also seen in the slow section of this toccata, confirms a tonality while also bringing the rhythmic motion to a stop.

EXAMPLE 3.29 Bach's toccata in D major, BWV 912.

D minor, BWV 913

Seen in Example 3.30 and also commencing with a single line, the D minor toccata establishes the tonic before moving through a complete circle of fifths, all within its first two measures. Two measures of tonic and dominant follow, mostly expressed in arpeggios. The sixth measure is a passage which uses all three forms of the minor scale during its short life. The next five measures use neighboring tones to fill in the sixteenth-note rhythm, similar to the D major toccata, but here with an actively changing harmony. As before, the secondary dominant sets up a conclusion on the dominant. Observations:

1. Single-line versions of the circle of fifths (C5) could be very useful in many improvisational situations.

2. If extending the tonic alone does not seem interesting enough, the improviser can let the tonic argue back and forth with the dominant for a long time instead, like a series of TDOs.

3. Another technique for prolonging a harmony is to use its neighboring tones for rhythmic and melodic interest.

EXAMPLE 3.30   Bach's toccata in D minor, BWV 913.

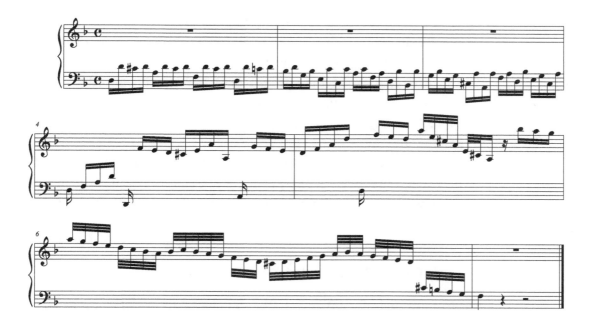

EXAMPLE 3.31   Bach's toccata in E minor, BWV 914.

E minor, BWV 914

As we see in Example 3.31, this toccata opening stands apart due its lack of virtuosity. Instead of brilliant passagework it presents an ominously repeated bass

note, answered each time by a tenor line. Then follows a series of FXB chords, a long dominant pedal, and a long tonic pedal. Observations:

1. The opening bass motive is interesting because it has a three-note anacrusis, as if to say, "And go to there," which is more engaging than a single note saying merely "there."

2. The three FXB passages are patterned: each moves downward to a temporary arrival, then up a step to commence moving again. The "interrupted" or staggered movement of fauxbourdon is more interesting that plain motion by step.

3. The final two measures again elaborate the tonic harmony (now in E major) by neighboring tones, which creates a sense of melodic movement which is more interesting than simple assertion of the tonic triad.

G minor, BWV 915

Refer to Example 3.32 for this piece. The four-measure introduction appears with triplets as the rhythmic division. Measures 1–2 occupy themselves with a rapid TDO, trading harmonies on every triplet. The third measure makes a Quiescenza-like motion toward the subdominant, while the fourth is comprised mostly of plagal motion between iv and i. The short opening concludes with a quick imperfect cadence as the next section, a chorale, begins. Observations:

1. The triplet is useful to the improviser because it can outline a triad or fill in a third with a passing tone. Triplets stay neatly within specific harmonies, whereas four sixteenths, if played stepwise in a row, outline a fourth and may easily take the performer outside the bounds of a single chord.

2. Once again we see that tonic-dominant "argument" can go on indefinitely, and really functions as a more elaborate way of prolonging the tonic.

EXAMPLE 3.32   Bach's toccata in G minor, BWV 915.

3. Plagal motion, that is, back and forth between i and iv, is another form of prolonging the tonic.

G major, BWV 916

We will study the first movement of the G major toccata in greater depth and take some of its building blocks for our own use. Refer to Example 3.33. The G major is uniquely instructive for the improviser because even though Bach

EXAMPLE 3.33   Bach's toccata in G major, BWV 916.

EXAMPLE 3.34   Scrambled opening of the Bach G major toccata.

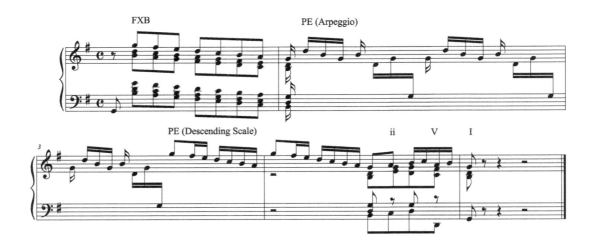

created it out of fairly obvious building blocks, yet the resulting composition is interesting and satisfying as a coherent musical statement. We will observe and steal building blocks from several of its passages.

The opening uses four building blocks: three to prolong the tonic harmony, and one cadence. The descending scale and arpeggiation could both be considered forms of PE, which we have discussed already. These, together with the subsequent FXB, all serve to extend I. Interestingly, these building blocks are interchangeable; we could switch the order of these three opening gestures and the music would still work, as long as we proceed to the cadence after the third building block. Example 3.34 shows an alternate version of the opening, with the building blocks in a scrambled order.

EXERCISE: Using the opening building blocks, improvise short passages in various keys. Use two different PEs, a FXB, and a cadence. Try the blocks in different orders, but always put the cadence last. Is it possible, after using all three (but before the cadence), to go back and repeat one of them? What alterations are required to play in minor keys? Example 3.35 shows two possible solutions for this exercise, one minor and one major.

Refer to Example 3.33 again. Starting in measure 5, we hear a pattern that alternates I and V. The pattern is invertible (i.e., the hands trade parts), as seen in measure 6. Playing material over again, but traded between the hands, sounds familiar enough to make sense but different enough to be interesting. (Even playing identical material one octave up or down can be enough to justify its repeat.) We could think of this as a special version of the TDO, with the hands trading material. Example 3.36 shows a few ideas for creating these.

EXERCISE: Play the TDO from Example 3.33. Transpose to several other keys. Try those in Example 3.36, and then make up some of your own. See if your TDOs will allow for inversion. An easy way to make your TDO invertible is to use imperfect consonances (thirds, sixths, and tenths) in parallel motion

EXAMPLE 3.35   Solutions for improvisation plan.

combined with a static note on 5. (Note how this is essentially the same as the P10 building block.)

The TDO ends on V, followed by a confirmation of that tonality by means of a quick cadence. And here is something very interesting: upon arrival in the dominant key, the piece starts over again verbatim: all the same material in the same order. (Note that the meter is "off" by half a measure. Composers of the eighteenth century treated the first and third beats of common meter as interchangeable downbeats; either one could be considered the rhythmically strong moment of the measure. If you compare the opening in G major with this restatement in D, you will notice the visual oddity of all the material shifted half a bar, and yet it does not sound rhythmically off-kilter.) Here we may observe yet one more technique for "getting away" with repeating material: do everything all over again, not an octave up or down, but this time in a different key.

EXAMPLE 3.36   Example amples of Tonic-Dominant Oscillations.

EXERCISE: Create a short piece using two PEs, FXB, and a cadence. Instead of ending at the cadence, continue the music with a TDO. Extend the TDO pattern by transposing it up or down one octave, or inverting it. Then create a cadence in the dominant. With the dominant tonicized, continue your improvisation, repeating all your previous material in the new key and concluding with a cadence in the dominant.

So far we have found four building blocks in the G major toccata: PE, FXB, ii-V-I cadence, and TDO. We will now add another.

In the middle of measure 13 (Example 3.33) a new event appears. This particular sequence is called the $^6_3$-$^4_2$ because those are the intervals above the bass. It is also known as tied bass. Example 3.37 shows the inner workings of this sequence as well as a few possible keyboard textures.

EXERCISE: Learn to play the $^6_3$-$^4_2$, starting with the examples in Example 3.37. Transpose them. Then invent your own $^6_3$-$^4_2$ patterns.

In the G major toccata, the $^6_3$-$^4_2$ serves as a prolongation of tonality. Whatever key we are in, the sequence will drag it out, after which it connects with a cadence. In order to use it as a building block, then, we need to learn how to launch and exit this sequence.

The sequence must begin on a first inversion chord (or, as eighteenth-century musicians would call it, a chord of the sixth). The starting chord of the sequence may be a chord you were already on, or a chord that naturally follows in a good stylistic progression. Sometimes Bach starts this sequence using the

EXAMPLE 3.37   Example amples of the $^6_3$-$^4_2$ sequence.

same chord he just played, and other times he jumps to a new (but harmonically plausible) chord. If you jump to something inappropriate, your ear will tell you immediately!

EXERCISE: Improvise a toccata by deploying two PEs and one FXB. Launch $^6_3$-$^4_2$ and allow it to descend to a tonic chord. Conclude with a cadence. Do this in several different keys.

Though Bach does not use his sequence to change key in this toccata, we know from previous material in this book (and from studying lots of music) that sequences are ideal vehicles for moving to a new tonality. As you recall, we may introduce the leading tone of the new key at any appropriate point within the sequence. Then we may exit the sequence and confirm the new key with a cadence. This will allow us to extend our toccatas into a variety of harmonic areas while continuing to use the same limited number of building blocks.

EXERCISE: Following the plans given here, improvise complete toccatas using the following building blocks: PE, FXB, TDO, $^6_3$-$^4_2$, and the cadence. The plans are rather long; you will probably need to work out them in shorter sections before playing them all the way through. Example 3.38 shows a possible solution for the major key plan.

For major keys:

Key Area: I
PEs and FXB in any order
Cadence in I
TDO in I
$^6_3$-$^4_2$ Sequence modulating to vi
Key Area: vi
PEs, TDO, and FXB in any order
Cadence in vi
$^6_3$-$^4_2$ modulating to V
Key Area: V
PEs and FXB in any order
TDO in V
Cadence in V
$^6_3$-$^4_2$ modulating to I
Key Area: I
PEs and FXB in any order
Cadence in I

For minor keys:

Key Area: i
PEs and FXB in any order
Cadence in i
$^6_3$-$^4_2$ modulating to III
Key Area: III
PEs and FXB in any order
Cadence in III
$^6_3$-$^4_2$ modulating to v

EXAMPLE 3.38.1 AND 3.38.2 Solution for the improvisation plan.

EXAMPLE 3.38.1 AND 3.38.2   Continued

Key Area: v

PEs and FXB in any order

Cadence in v (but arrive on major V instead)

$^6_3$-$^4_2$ modulating to i

Key Area: i

PEs and FXB in any order

Cadence in i

EXERCISE: Develop and perform a variety of your own toccata plans using various combinations of building blocks.

In your zibaldone, create collections of the building blocks from this chapter. Invent some of your own or find them in the repertoire. Design your own toccata plans using as many building blocks as you like.

Chapter 4

The Rule of the Octave

Most eighteenth-century treatises begin with intervals, followed by cadences. As soon as the student could tell the difference between consonance and dissonance and manage a few variants of V-I, the next assignment was to master the Rule of the Octave (RO). The RO is a set of principles for harmonizing a scale in the bass. The system provides a set of intervals for upper voices to match each scale degree in the bass. The RO is not the only way to harmonize a bass scale, but it is the most broadly applicable, and therefore constantly useful for the improviser. While RO can harmonize a leaping bass, this chapter will consider stepwise motion only. RO was so commonly taught that its sounds informed the development of music for centuries.

In its simplest form the RO gives chords of the fifth to ① and ⑤ in the bass. Every other bass note receives a chord of the sixth. Example 4.1 shows the simple form of the RO.

EXERCISE: Play the ascending RO pattern shown in the example. Transpose it to several other major keys. Practice until it is familiar enough that you can play it at a moderate tempo, without hesitation.

The RO includes two changes when descending in major. ⑥ takes a raised sixth. (We could also explain this as a secondary dominant.) ④ is also different when descending; it now takes a second and fourth, or what some call a third inversion of the dominant. See Example 4.2.

EXERCISE: Play the descending RO pattern shown in Example 4.2. Transpose it to several other major keys. Practice it until it is familiar enough that you can play it at a moderate tempo, without hesitation.

We might call this *Simple RO* because it uses only three voices. It is possible to improvise using Simple RO because it is convenient for a three-voice figuration context: one need not add or throw away any notes, as every pitch from the RO will fit the figuration. In fact, ascending and descending (or vice versa) through Simple RO, with appropriate figuration, will make a nice, complete prelude.

EXAMPLE 4.1   The simple rule of the octave, ascending.

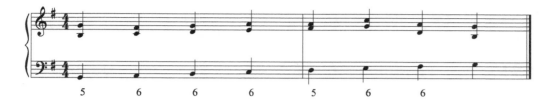

EXAMPLE 4.2   The simple rule of the octave, descending.

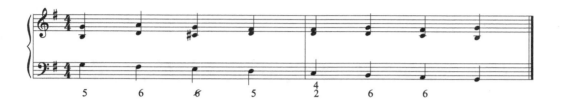

EXERCISE: Improvise figuration preludes using Simple RO. Try various meters. It does not matter whether you start with ascent or descent. Example 4.3 shows Simple RO in block chord form and then provides two possible solutions in figuration. Notice that the second solution (in B♭) stretches each chord into a full measure, resulting in a surprisingly long piece generated from such basic material.

In minor keys, Simple RO needs a few important alterations. When ascending, the bass scale takes the melodic (raised) form. When descending, the bass again follows the melodic scale (now lowered). Earlier musicians would have given both ⑦ and ⑥ thirds and sixths in descending form. Later, in what we might call galant style, ⑥ takes a raised sixth, resulting in an augmented sixth interval. While Bach certainly used the augmented sixth at times, to some listeners the sound of the augmented sixth may be associated with the galant and classical era, not with the Baroque. In my opinion, RO without raised sixth sounds older and more German; adding the raised sixth sounds more modern and Italian. Improvisers may use either version depending on the sound and era they wish to evoke.

In Example 4.4, the galant version (with raised sixth) is shown, followed by a version without the raised sixth. In this second version, once voice is sometimes delayed to avoid fifths. We may call this version the *passacaglia* as this progression often appears in sorrowful music.

EXERCISE: Practice minor Simple RO. Improvise pieces using figuration. Transpose to several keys. Use both the galant and passacaglia versions and listen carefully to the difference.

Simple RO is useful as a stepping stone for learning, but as soon as you have mastered it, you should move on. In the "full" version of RO, ① and ⑤ are

EXAMPLE 4.3   Simple RO with figuration examples.

EXAMPLE 4.4   The Simple RO in minor.

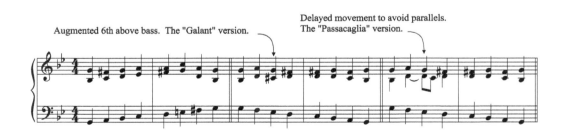

Augmented 6th above bass. The "Galant" version.

Delayed movement to avoid parallels.
The "Passacaglia" version.

EXAMPLE 4.5   The Full RO.

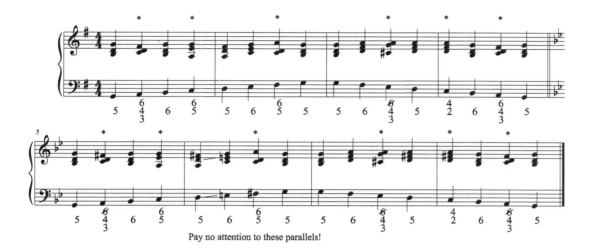

Pay no attention to these parallels!

still the only bass notes that take chords of the fifth. However, several other chords get an additional note. In Example 4.5, the new additions are marked with asterisks.

This is the full version of the RO. Historical models do not agree on what to do about the soprano. Fedele Fenaroli, for example, taught versions for all three positions of the soprano, starting with ❶, ❸, and ❺ in the top voice. Fenaroli kept the movement of the soprano very conservative, moving only one step up and down from the starting note. François Campion, who coined the term "Rule of the Octave," advocated a much freer soprano line. Other writers have their own approach to the soprano. We can conclude that historically speaking, the soprano need not follow any particular melodic line. Besides, inventing your own soprano line is excellent improvisation practice.

Many treatises (such as Fenaroli's) show RO with a varying texture of three to five voices, although it is possible to represent all the sonorities required by the treatises while consistently using four voices. In Example 4.5, four voices are present throughout.

In four-voice keyboard texture we may disregard minor voice-leading concerns involving inner voices; eighteenth-century masters certainly did. In vocal or instrumental contexts, these matters would be solved through voice-crossing. On the piano one cannot hear whether voices have crossed. As long as the outer voice-leading is good and the inner voices support the correct harmony, the parts are usually considered correct.

EXERCISE: Learn the full RO, ascending and descending, major and minor. Transpose to other keys. Mastering RO in every key will take some time. Start with the keys up to three accidentals in each direction.

EXERCISE: The four-voice RO allows for more interesting figurations, especially when the bass note has the option of bouncing between octaves.

Develop some figurations that fit four voices, and apply them to RO in short improvised preludes. Example 4.6 provides two ideas. Try various meters. You can move in quick harmonic rhythm, touching on each chord only for a beat, or stretch each chord into a complete measure or more.

The soprano may begin on any position of the first chord. (Remember, "position" refers to what note is in the soprano, and is not to be confused with inversion.) I do not think it is necessary to learn every position of RO in a precise, memorized manner. As long as you can avoid parallel fifths and octaves between soprano and bass, making adjustments in the direction of the soprano as you play, you need not stick with a single version. If you begin ascending in first position (with the soprano on ❶), the soprano cannot proceed to ❷ on the next chord, since that would create parallel octaves with the bass. Instead, the soprano could descend to ❼ or leap down to ❺, or leap up to ❺.

EXERCISE: Practice RO using only Example 4.7 as a guide. Begin in first position, and then try starting with second and third positions. Avoid parallel fifths and octaves between soprano and bass. Note any voice-leading problems that result from your choices. Try to create a logical and pleasing contour in the soprano line. Add figuration. Transpose.

EXAMPLE 4.6   RO with figurations.

EXAMPLE 4.7   Major and minor RO for practicing.

You should memorize RO in major and minor. Its harmonic patterns are pervasive throughout most styles of music, and thorough mastery will provide you with a lifetime of fluent musicianship.

Counterintuitively, finding examples of a complete stepwise RO passage (either ascending or descending) in written music is very difficult. Given that most pedagogues emphasized the primacy of the RO, it may seem odd that they did not often use it in its entirety in composition. I suspect they avoided it for the same reason a literature professor would not begin his own novel with "Once upon a time." Too obvious.

We do observe shorter segments of the RO in written music all the time. Example 4.8 shows a passage from J. S. Bach's Prelude in C minor, BWV 546, in which the bass falls from ⑤ to ① using textbook RO harmonization. The norm, it seems, was to use shorter segments of RO. Passages built on ①-⑤ or ③-⑥ are extremely common, for instance. A rare instance of a complete RO appears in Händel's organ concerto in F, Op. 4 no. 5, shown (in reduction) in Example 4.9. Still, complete ROs in written music are so unusual that I could not find any examples without the help of expert musicologists!

However, I suggest that it was probably a near-universal practice to use the complete stepwise RO for improvising in the eighteenth century. C. P. E. Bach advised novice improvisers that if no other ideas were forthcoming, they could improvise upon a scale. He meant a scale in the bass, harmonized by the RO. C. P. E. Bach taught and used the RO extensively; in his *Essay on*

EXAMPLE 4.8   From Bach's BWV 546.

EXAMPLE 4.9   From Händel's Op. 4 no. 5.

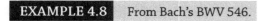

Complete Ascending RO

the True Art of Playing Keyboard Instruments he teaches the standard RO and offers many extra variants, with secondary dominants, chromatic motion, and nonharmonic tones. He certainly advocated its wide use in extemporaneous playing. Therefore, the practice of improvising "upon a scale" is historically rooted, even though we don't find many such passages in written music.

The RO is useful for many forms of improvisation, including the unmeasured prelude. We have already touched on this style in the chapter on toccata when we used Whole Note Chords (WNC) as building blocks. The unmeasured prelude traces its origins at least to Louis Couperin (1626–1661) who wrote down his pieces in a strikingly unorthodox manner, using only whole notes and long sweeping ties. By the mid-eighteenth century the practice of presenting complete harmonies in whole note chords was commonplace. Example 4.10 shows a selection in this style from Händel's Prelude HWV 568.

RO is easily adapted for unmeasured prelude. As long as the outer parts use good voice-leading, the inner parts need only conform to the correct harmony and may disregard questions of parallels or doublings. In fact, if one reads through numerous unmeasured preludes, one realizes that the strategy is to fill both hands with as many chord tones as possible.

The style of performance is very free. The player usually arpeggiates each chord from the bottom up, and then back down again. One may arpeggiate each chord two or even three times, and may use various figuration patterns to break up the chord. The arpeggio should be articulate; the goal is not to get through as fast as possible but to allow the listener to hear the details of each harmony. One may vary the speed of the arpeggiation. It is possible to pause at moments of piquancy. You should be guided by sense of drama and rhetoric.

A short prelude may consist of nothing more than a simple traversal of the ascending or descending version, in major or minor. Example 4.11 conveys the

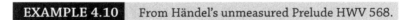

EXAMPLE 4.10   From Händel's unmeasured Prelude HWV 568.

EXAMPLE 4.11   Ascending RO in unmeasured shorthand.

general idea. Once you know RO in every key, tossing off a short unmeasured prelude takes no effort at all.

EXERCISE: Improvise unmeasured preludes in various keys using RO in arpeggiated WNCs.

We can develop the use of RO within unmeasured preludes to a higher degree. J. C. Fischer provides an interesting example in which he combines WNC with Patterned Elaboration (PE), just as we saw with Sarti in the toccata chapter. Fischer's piece, the Prelude from his suite in D, appears in Example 4.12. The combination of these two textures makes for interesting contrast and musical drama.

EXERCISE: Write out a plan for a piece like Fischer's that combines the WNC style of unmeasured prelude with PE. Don't notate the music; just write down general directions such as a bass line with figures, when to use the different styles, and so on. During the WNC sections, use RO. Choose some other progressions to use for PEs. Move among several different keys. Next, try improvising a piece without a written plan.

After mastering RO, we may modify it through nonharmonic tones. Suspensions add interest and drama to the progression, and also help disguise

EXAMPLE 4.12   J. C. F. Fischer, Prelude from the Suite in D major.

the formulaic nature of RO improvisations. (A good strategy for the improviser is to use very simple methods but hide the simplicity from the listener!)

We may suspend any upper voice within the RO, but I recommend starting with the top voice as it is easiest to track mentally. Look for a point within RO where the top voice will move up or down by step. When the voice ought to move, keep it on the old note and listen to the result. Then move it to the correct note. Example 4.13 demonstrates this procedure.

When playing in the arpeggiated style of the unmeasured prelude, the top note may be doubled lower in the chord. Doubling the suspension is fine in that situation. However, in figuration prelude style, voices are not normally doubled except for bass octaves. In figuration style, the suspension in the top voice should not appear elsewhere in the chord.

Example 4.14 shows Fenaroli's RO in first position in its original form and with added suspensions in the soprano on every chord change. Strictly speaking, the nonharmonic tone on the downbeat of the last measure is an accented passing tone, not a suspension (for those who take note of such distinctions).

EXERCISE: Work your way through major and minor RO patterns, starting in various positions of the first chord. Note where interesting and satisfying suspensions may occur, and remember these for later use in improvisation. Work on both ascending and descending forms. Transpose.

EXERCISE: Plan a longer and more elaborate piece using RO in both unmeasured and figuration prelude styles, interspersed with PE episodes that use

EXAMPLE 4.13   RO with suspensions.

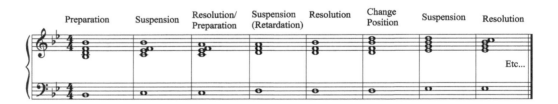

EXAMPLE 4.14   Adding suspensions to RO.

non-RO progressions. Move among at least three different keys before returning to the tonic. Record yourself improvising the piece and review the recording to improve both your planning and execution.

As mentioned earlier, C. P. E. Bach taught RO along with many variants. Example 4.15 shows no fewer than 25 of his RO versions. Other teachers might not consider all these to be strictly RO. For instance, Fenaroli taught the third version (measure 3) as a separate, non-RO pattern. It does not matter whether we call these harmonizations RO or something else. The point is to study many different options for evoking music from a simple bass scale.

EXERCISE: Choose a few of C. P. E. Bach's scale harmonizations and realize them at the piano. Use them to improvise short pieces. Write down his RO versions in your zibaldone for further study.

EXAMPLE 4.15   C. P. E. Bach's RO variants.

Chapter 5

Diminution

Eighteenth-century music is made of harmonic patterns. However, music is rarely a mere series of chords; that would be boring. Individual voices within the chords are broken up and differentiated into separate lines. Vertically considered, a note is merely a chord factor or a nonharmonic tone. Horizontally, though, it is part of a coherent melodic line.

Historians tell us that counterpoint came first and harmony followed as a result. In other words, musicians of the past developed independent counterpointing lines that sounded good together, and the resulting combinations of sound were accepted and called chords. Over time chords were standardized into the triadic system of harmony we know today.

During improvisation, however, this process may happen in reverse order. Today's musicians tend to think in terms of chord progressions more readily than counterpointing lines. This is a result of the fact that for most of us, our educational experiences placed far more emphasis on harmonic analysis than contrapuntal awareness. Fortunately, it is possible to learn to play contrapuntally by taking advantage of our relative fluency with chord progressions.

One way to approach this challenge is to choose in advance what chord progression to use, and decide later (even in the midst of playing) how to differentiate the voices within those chords into independent lines. We may achieve this goal through the use of *diminution*.

Diminution fills in gaps between longer notes with shorter notes, thus creating a flowing line with its own distinct character. By practicing various diminution patterns we may acquire the ability to fill in gaps of any melodic interval. Example 5.1 shows sample diminution patterns that cover intervals from a unison to a sixth, ascending and descending.

EXERCISE: Example 5.2 shows unaccompanied melodies for each hand alone, made mostly of quarter notes. Based on the intervals between notes, add diminutions to each line. Each quarter note in the example will become the first

EXAMPLE 5.1 Diminution patterns for each interval.

of four sixteenths; you need to fill in the other three. Initially you may find it helpful to write out your solutions. As soon as you can, stop writing and make them up in real time as you play through Example 5.2. Next, write down some familiar tunes that are made primarily of uniform rhythmic values, and improvise diminutions on them. Be sure to use many different keys and to practice with each hand separately. Consult the chart of diminutions (Example 5.1) whenever you are unsure how to fill an interval. The examples in the chart are not the only way to fill in intervals; make up some of your own diminutions. By the time you are done practicing, you should have memorized at least one way to cover every interval up to a sixth, ascending and descending, in each hand. Example 5.3 provides possible solutions for the first two tunes from 5.2.

EXERCISE: Examples 5.4 through 5.8 show short pieces in two voices. Play each as written, then again with diminutions in the right hand while the left remains unaltered. Go slowly so you have time to choose a diminution. Then go back and apply diminutions to the left hand, leaving the right hand as quarter notes. Finally, let the hands take turns using diminutions, so that at any given moment one hand is playing quarters and the other sixteenths. Using this diminution trading technique, you can develop many variations on

EXAMPLE 5.2   Melodies for diminution practice.

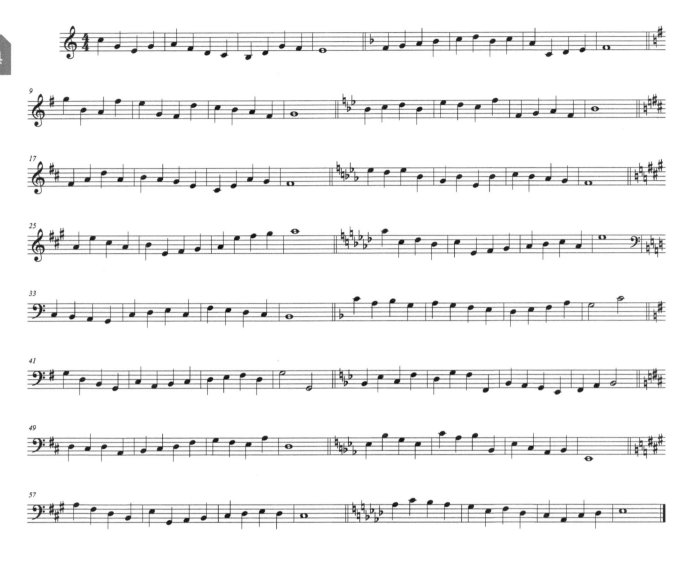

EXAMPLE 5.3   Diminution solutions.

EXAMPLE 5.4 Exercise for diminution practice.

EXAMPLE 5.5 Exercise for diminution practice.

EXAMPLE 5.6 Exercise for diminution practice.

EXAMPLE 5.7 Exercise for diminution practice.

EXAMPLE 5.8 Exercise for diminution practice.

each piece. Example 5.9 illustrates diminution trading applied to Example 5.8. Notice that in ¾ time, trading on every beat (as in measures 5 and 6) creates a sense of hemiola.

We now move from two voices to three. In eighteenth-century keyboard music, the rhythmic activity of individual voices is inversely proportional to the number of voices present. This is due in part to the limitations of the hand, which cannot play multivoice passages of infinite complexity, but also because the musical "space" must not be too crowded. Like a packed dance floor, more

EXAMPLE 5.9 Diminution trading.

EXAMPLE 5.10 Simplified chorales.

participants means less freedom of movement for each. When playing in three voices, then, the improviser should feel no obligation to keep all of them in constant activity through diminution.

EXERCISE: Example 5.10 presents two simplified chorales of J. S. Bach, reduced to three voices. Play each as written, then try adding diminutions to the top voice. Go back through again and do the same to the middle and bottom voices. Apply diminution trading to the examples, creating several versions by scrambling the order in which each voice receives diminution. Finally, go back and transpose the material to other keys.

Example 5.11 depicts a 5-6 ascending sequence, first in unadorned notes, then three more times to show diminutions in each voice. Because sequences move by pattern, the same intervals recur. This makes diminutions easier. Example 5.11 only moves by unisons and seconds, so you only need two types of diminution to solve the whole thing.

EXAMPLE 5.11 Ascending 5-6 sequence with diminutions.

EXERCISE: Play the sequence in Example 5.11. Apply diminutions to each voice, using something other than what is provided in the example. Then try diminution trading between voices. Note that depending on which voice is applying diminutions, the middle voice might need to be traded between the hands. This is a normal adjustment you should expect to make when improvising diminutions. Now look at Example 5.12, which is a descending 7-6 sequence. Practice some diminutions on this sequence which are different from those written. Transpose to different keys.

Example 5.13 shows a bass sequence that descends a third and rises a second, followed by a version with diminution trading. Notice that the sequence is undermined by the fact that the pattern of diminution trading does not match the pattern of the sequence itself. In order for the sequence to sound right, everything has to happen according to the pattern. That means that each time the pattern repeats, each voice must use exactly the same diminutions in the same place. This does not mean that the example is wrong in terms of voice-leading, nor that it is musically illegitimate, but only that it has lost its character as a sequence.

EXAMPLE 5.12 Descending 7-6 sequence with diminutions.

EXAMPLE 5.13 Incorrect and correct matching of diminution to sequence.

Sequence sabotaged by non-patterned diminutions

A better version

The third version in the example shows a better solution. (The last diminution in the soprano must be altered to avoid cadencing on a dissonance. This is a normal and expected adjustment in eighteenth-century music.)

In the sequence in Example 5.13, the pattern is two chords long. That means that you may apply diminutions to the first and second chords as you wish, but after that, the pattern is set and must be maintained.

EXERCISE: Solve the sequence in Example 5.13 with several different versions of diminution trading, while preserving the integrity of the sequence. Transpose.

EXAMPLE 5.14 Simplified sarabande of J. S. Bach.

We will now add diminutions to some more nonsequential three-voice progressions. A good place to start is the style the sarabande, wherein individual lines within a three-voice texture receive occasional elaboration by diminution, but the texture as a whole does not get too thick with constantly running notes. The sarabandes from the French suites of J. S. Bach (BWV 812–817) are particularly suitable for this purpose. Example 5.14 shows a simplified version of the opening eight measures of the sarabande from the G major French suite.

EXERCISE: Apply 16th-note diminutions to the sarabande in Example 5.14. Take each voice in turn and then trade diminutions. When applying diminutions to a half note, treat it as two quarters and thus use two successive diminutions, the first of which must span a unison; the second will connect to the following written note. Example 5.15 shows two possible solutions.

Obviously, diminutions are not always sixteenths, but may take any form appropriate to the style and texture of the piece. One of the simplest diminutions is a note broken in two (e.g., a quarter becomes two eighths) and the second note serves as a passing or neighbor tone. In compound meters, three-note diminutions will be ubiquitous. Example 5.16 shows some compound diminutions for various intervals. No chart can list all possible diminutions in all possible rhythmic contexts. You should strive to create your own diminutions, in various meters, in real time.

EXERCISE: Go back to the simplified sarabande in Example 5.14 and apply diminutions of various rhythms. If the musical context permits, some moments may need no diminution at all. In the sarabande style, the rhythm can be highly variegated; try filling thirds with simple stepwise eighth notes, fourths with an occasional triplet, and so on. Of course, you can also add ornaments such as mordants, turns, and trills. Example 5.17 shows one possible solution which includes a few ambitious diminutions, including the use of accented passing tones and faster note groups.

Applying diminutions can sometimes create voice-leading hazards. For example, it is permissible for two voices simultaneously to receive diminution in parallel motion between imperfect consonances, but not between octaves and fifths. When using diminutions in two voices at the same time, you are safest if the interval between the voices is imperfect (thirds, sixths, tenths) and the

EXAMPLE 5.15   Sarabande with two diminution solutions.

EXAMPLE 5.16   Diminutions in compound time.

diminutions match exactly. One can even get in trouble applying diminutions to parallel tenths if two different kinds of diminution are used. This is one reason diminution trading is so useful: one is less likely to create undesirable parallels. Example 5.18 illustrates these points.

EXAMPLE 5.17   Sarabande with ornaments and diminutions.

EXAMPLE 5.18   Problems and solutions with diminutions in two voices.

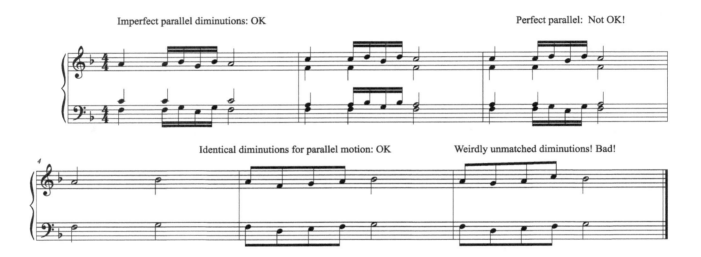

Example 5.19 illustrates a simple (but extremely useful) diminution strategy. We may call it *rhythmic activation*. A longer note can be turned into a dotted (or double-dotted) rhythm, and the note restruck near the end of its duration, just before moving to the next note. This technique is easy to apply in real time, and has no effect on the overall voice-leading because it introduces no new pitches. Still, rhythmic activation creates a sense of difference between voices, transforming the listener's perception of the texture from chordal to polyphonic. The French overture style makes extensive use of this technique.

Another element of the French overture style lies halfway between rhythmic activation and diminution. In this technique, the principal note is connected to the following note by diminution, but the diminution is delayed until near the end of the beat, and then deployed in very fast rhythm. There is no official name for this procedure, but we may call it *dotted diminution*. Example 5.20 provides a few instances.

EXAMPLE 5.19 Rhythmic activation.

EXAMPLE 5.20 Examples of dotted diminution.

EXAMPLE 5.21   Adding diminutions to familiar progressions.

EXERCISE: Practice short chord progressions with rhythmic activations and dotted diminutions. Any stylistically appropriate progression will do, but you may find it easiest to use familiar patterns such as Page One, C5, Descending 7-6, and so on. Activate one voice at a time, and trade between all voices frequently. Do this in many different keys. Example 5.21 provides some guidance.

ii-V-I with Diminutions

Jazz musicians sometimes speak of "shedding ii-V-Is." Shedding is short for woodshedding, a reference to the unfortunate practice of taking an ill-behaved child behind the woodshed for a disciplinary beating. In the present context it means practicing a skill (perhaps with violent intensity) until it behaves as desired. The ii-V-I comprises a significant portion of the standard jazz repertoire. Shedding ii-V-Is means rehearsing various solo lines that harmonize with that progression until it becomes effortless to make them up spontaneously. Because of the ubiquity of that chord pattern, fluent improvising over the ii-V-I equates to fluent improvising in jazz. If you command the ii-V-I, you command everything.

Interestingly, a similar approach appears in the *Nova Instructio* (1670–1677) of Spiridion á Monte Carmelo (1615–1685). The *Nova Instructio* was a practical treatise to help church keyboard musicians acquire improvisational abilities. Spiridion starts by requiring his readers to memorize a V-I cadence

EXAMPLE 5.22   Progressions for diminution shedding.

in G major. Then follow 72 examples of the same cadence elaborated with diminutions, ornamentation, and various strategies of decoration and extension. The underlying cadence never changes. The idea behind Spiridion's exhaustive and exhausting book is to fill one's head with so many ways to play cadences that eventually one can just rattle them off without any trouble. Spiridion understood that if you command the V-I, you command everything. And the way to get there is to shed.

We will now shed some ii-V-Is.

EXERCISE: Example 5.22 depicts some ii-V-I and ii°-V-i progressions in various positions and inversions. Shed these progressions extensively in all major and minor keys in the following ways:

1. Apply diminutions to one voice at a time;
2. Try diminution-trading in various combinations;
3. Play in compound meters, using diminutions based on three-note groups;
4. Use rhythmic activation, adding no new pitches;
5. Use dotted diminution in one voice at a time;
6. Use dotted diminution trading.

Example 5.23 shows a few solutions out of the infinite number of possibilities. Remember: if you command the ii-V-I, you command everything. You will be able to use these cadences with every kind of eighteenth-century improvisation.

Compound Melody

Compound melody consists of a single moving line seeming to imply two or more voices, usually by leaping between registers "occupied" by these imaginary multiple parts. No clear distinction separates compound melody from

EXAMPLE 5.23 Examples of ii-V-I progressions with diminutions.

"real" polyphony, and on paper we often encounter passages that could be considered as either one. Example 5.24 shows the opening bar of John Loeillet's A major allemande, first in original form and then in my altered notation. The second version has changed multivoice notation to single and vice-versa, and yet the two versions would be played more or less the same. In fact, many keyboard passages in eighteenth-century music could be notated in various ways, showing a greater or lesser number of voices, without changing how we play it.

Eighteenth-century keyboard music is surprisingly casual about keeping track of voices. Perhaps I got the idea that all voices are constantly monitored and accounted-for from part-writing in theory class, where it is unlawful to make the tenor vanish from time to time, convenient though that may be. It is true that fugue expositions are usually strict; some even show rests for each voice in empty measures. However, once things get underway, the rules relax considerably, and very few eighteenth-century keyboard pieces—even the fugues of Bach, who is the strictest of all—maintain a precise number of voices from beginning to end.

Of course, choral and instrumental music must remember its own forces and to employ them at reasonable intervals; keyboard music carries no such obligation. While a piece may be generally conceived as two, three, or four voices, no one cries foul (or even notices) when a four-voice piece drops to two for a while, or a two-part composition ends triumphantly in a six-voice chord.

Example 5.25 illustrates a few passages that one may imagine as polyphonic or compound.

In improvisation, compound melody may be used similarly to diminution. Diminution transforms block chords into polyphonic textures; compound melody can do the same thing. Example 5.26 shows a passage (derived from a Händel prelude) in block chords, then with diminutions, and finally elaborated by compound melody. The strategy behind compound melody is to touch on all

EXAMPLE 5.24   Beginning of Loeillet's allemande in original and altered notation.

EXAMPLE 5.25   Notation of polyphony and compound melody.

EXAMPLE 5.26 Example of development from block chords to polyphony to compound melody.

important chord tones but weave them into a flowing monophonic line, which may also include nonharmonic tones.

Unlike figuration prelude, compound melody need not keep a completely consistent pattern of figuration. At the same time, a compound melodic line that hits all the important chord tones but shows no rhyme or reason in its pattern will sound wrong.

The advantage of compound melody in improvisation is that the performer may evoke a full harmonic landscape using only a monophonic line, while providing a constant rhythmic texture.

EXERCISE: Go back to Examples 5.10 through 5.13. Create compound melodic lines for the right hand by combining the two top voices into a single part.

To conclude this chapter we will revisit some of the formulae we used when improvising figuration preludes. As you recall, we learned progressions in three voices before adding figuration. Those same three-voice progressions will work exceedingly well for practicing diminution. (While figuration and diminution may seem superficially similar in that they both take an underlying chord progression and make it texturally and rhythmically more interesting, diminution is the more sophisticated of the two techniques because it actually connects the successive tones within each voice in a coherent melodic manner.)

Following is one of the minor key plans from the figuration prelude chapter. We will use it as a template for adding diminutions. Before proceeding, you may wish to review all the terms from that chapter.

Quiescenza in i
Desc 7-6 to v
Cadence in v
Page One in v
Asc 5-6 to III
Cadence in III
Quiescenza in III
Desc 7-6 to i
Converging Cadence in i
Quiescenza in i

EXERCISE: Choose a minor key. Work out the preceding plan in three-voice block chords. If necessary, write out the chords. Begin playing through the progression, adding diminutions to the soprano only. Go slowly and be very patient. Next, go through again, this time applying diminutions to the middle voice. Next, the bass. After that, try diminution trading, rhythmic activation, and dotted diminution. Try various meters and of course, several different keys. Example 5.27 shows the minor key plan with each element labelled. Example 5.28 illustrates one possible solution—an ambitious one—using all of the techniques at once. The harmonic progression and voice-leading of Example 5.28 match those of 5.27 measure for measure so you may compare the two and note how each technique has been applied.

EXAMPLE 5.27   Minor key plan.

EXAMPLE 5.28   Solution for minor key plan.

A thorough understanding of diminution, diminution trading, rhythmic activation, and dotted diminution allows the improviser to create a highly detailed, complex, and interesting piece of music from a very simple underlying progression.

In your zibaldone, create a chart of your own diminutions, connecting notes of intervals from a unison up to a sixth.

Chapter 6

Variations

As we study works of the eighteenth century for insight into improvisation, we note that certain pieces disclose the composer's method of construction rather obviously. Compositions in variation form are among the most approachable in this regard; a quick reading or hearing reveals how they work, and by implication, how the performer may learn to improvise them. Variations begin with brief thematic material and then expound upon that material in a clear, orderly, repetitive manner. Each variation can serve as a short lesson in improvisational strategy.

The variation form may appear by other names such as chaconne, passacaglia, doubles, or divisions on a ground. Despite stylistic differences, pieces under these titles all do the same thing: they develop a repeating bass line or chord progression.

The mental process of improvising in variation form resembles that of mid-twentieth-century jazz. As in jazz, variations provide an established chord progression that loops as many times as you like. You never have to solve the problem of what key you are in and what chord you are on, nor how many measures to allot to each harmonic event. If the theme involves a modulation, it will be brief and simple, and it will work the same way in each subsequent variation. For these reasons, improvising variations is an excellent way to gain confidence and fluency.

In this chapter we will investigate music of Händel and Witt, and appropriate some of their variation strategies in order to expand our own improvisational abilities.

Variations from the eighteenth century exhibit the following characteristics:

1. The theme appears first, and often consists of four or eight bars of music. The theme may be divided into two sections with repeats, but not necessarily. Any meter is possible, although the chaconne and passacaglia are often in $\frac{3}{4}$. The theme will emphasize a chord

progression or a bass line. It may include a melody that is lyrical or highly ornamented, but that is often a surface element and not the main point. The theme will begin on the tonic and conclude on the tonic (most commonly) or the dominant. Major and minor keys are equally common.

2. The bass line and chord progression may follow any pattern that fits within the specific number of measures. Händel's passacaglia in G minor (from the Suite HWV 432) follows a modified circle of fifths. Pachelbel's chaconne in F minor (T. 206) uses a stepwise descending bass, while his C major chaconne (T. 201) employs the ascending fifths pattern (named "Monte Romanesca" by Robert Gjerdingen). Alessandro Scarlatti's "Folia" variations follow a traditional progression that gives more or less equal time to the minor home key and its relative major.

3. Variations follow immediately after the statement of the theme. While the variations might make occasional reference to the theme's melody (even occasionally reiterating it verbatim), their primary business is to explore possibilities inherent in the bass line and chord progression.

4. Variations may be few or many. In Händel's pieces they range from two to 62.

5. The variations will have the same number of measures as the theme; important bass notes and harmonic events will appear in the same place in the variations as in the theme.

6. Generally, variations stay in the same key as the theme, although we will explore an exception to this later. The theme itself may be entirely diatonic or may include a brief tonicization of the dominant.

7. Variations may change tempo, although to do so is somewhat uncommon. If a tempo change occurs, it normally persists through several variations, creating a cohesive contrasting section, like a slow movement embedded within the composition. Meter changes are not common, although it's possible; Pachelbel changed meters many times in one chaconne (T. 201).

8. The variations may be loosely organized into sections. Frequently, the first few variations are somewhat understated, as though testing the waters, while later on the variations increase in drama and virtuosity. Groups of variations may "play off" the same idea for a while. Pieces in variation form often culminate with a few highly demonstrative, exciting variations—saving the best for last.

9. It is possible to restate the theme in its original form as a conclusion.

10. Chaconnes and passacaglias often emphasize the second beat of the measure with an agogic accent.

Variations tend to be predictable and uniform. Jazz pianist Brad Mehldau notes that this quality is both limiting and liberating:

> The impulse to constantly repeat the opening thematic material is, in itself, unintelligent and narratively shortsighted. One relinquishes any real possibility of structural development. Theme and variations take a proto-copy-paste approach, and in the literature of high Classicism, they have a unique identity—I think of them as the dumb-assed cousin of the other more exalted forms. Really, though, this cousin is more complex; he is more of an idiot-savant figure. For while he repeats the structure of his story over and over again, he uses his rich imaginative gift to fill it with something continuously new. Yes, the structure stays fixed, but once we are free from the burden of actual structural development, so many unusual and downright strange things can happen.

For the improviser, the very predictability and uniformity Mehldau decries are wonderfully helpful at the early stages of learning. The occasional monotony of variation form is our friend because it partly answers the improviser's constant question, "What should I do next?"

We now turn our attention to the chaconne in G with 62 Variations by Händel (HWV 442). Example 6.2 displays only the theme and selected variations discussed next, not the complete composition. You should refer to it constantly as you read the following descriptions.

The theme is eight bars long, venturing from tonic to mildly tonicized dominant before proceeding back home again. This slight emphasis on V in the middle of the theme will allow each variation, in its short lifespan, to feel like it had a chance to go somewhere. This same progression supports the aria in J. S. Bach's *Goldberg Variations*, which is why some call it the Goldberg Progression. The first four measures consist of descending Rule of the Octave (RO), and the second four measures are also derived from RO, ascending from ③ to ⑤ in the bass before cadencing on ①.

EXERCISE: Play the theme from HWV 442. Transpose it into several distant keys so that you truly understand its harmonic landscape.

We will not study every one of the 62 variations on this theme. (Indeed, listening to a complete performance is a bit of an ordeal, in my opinion.) However, we will look in depth at several of Händel's variations and consider what they may tell us about improvising.

EXERCISE: Compose your own eight-measure progression. Write this out as you will make reference to it often in the exercises that follow. Be sure it follows good voice-leading procedures, as faulty writing will come back to haunt you in every variation.

Variation 4 is a curiously plain version of the theme; it exists only as block chords. Notice the characteristic agogic accent on beat 2. The music seems to lean against the second beat ever so gently. From this variation we note that simplification is a valid form of improvisation. One can either elaborate the theme or one can simplify it. Eighteenth-century performers would likely have arpeggiated these chords for effect.

EXERCISE: Play Variation 4. Try it with different positions of the soprano and solve voice-leading issues that arise. Transpose it to several distant keys.

Variations 10 and 11 come as a pair, playing off the same rhythmic and textural idea. (In fact, the rhythmic idea continues through Variation 15.) On the downbeat in Variation 10 a chord establishes the harmony, after which the distinctive sixteenth-note neighbor gesture provides interest. Then follows arpeggiation of the currently active harmony. In order to improvise a variation like this, you must know the bass line and chord progression of the theme very well. You must also avoid clumsy parallels between the bass and the right hand's downbeat. If they move in parallel motion, the intervals should be imperfect consonances (thirds, sixths, and tenths). The arpeggiation is not in a consistent pattern and may be whatever fits the hand and sounds good.

Variation 11 is slightly easier because the left hand is more predictable regarding where the sixteenth-note gesture occurs and how the arpeggio works.

EXERCISE: Play Variations 10 and 11 in succession. Transpose them to different keys and play them together. Using your original progression, improvise two variations on it in the manner of Variations 10 and 11. Transpose your progression to several keys and improvise variations on it in each key.

Variations 19 and 21 will now seem simple by comparison. The improviser should take note that these plain textures are always available. I like to use them as emergency options when I need to play something easy and give myself a moment to think.

Variations 24–30 all employ repeated notes within the figuration. The advantage of repeated notes is that they cut down on the number of "new" notes you need to find. In Variation 24 the right hand needs to find only two or three pitches per measure, but may expand them into a six-note pattern. The same is true for the left hand in Variation 25. Throughout all these repeated-note variations, the repetition begins on a weak beat. It is also possible to change the pattern and commence repetition on a strong beat; the effect is very different.

The pattern starting in Variation 26 is especially clever. Using three of the same notes in a row allows for a fast rhythmic division in sixteenths but the improviser only needs to think of a few notes. Variation 29 demonstrates a nicely manageable version of this pattern in the right hand: only two pitches allow for the creation of brilliant figuration that fills an entire measure.

EXERCISE: Play variations 19, 21, and 24–30. Transpose them. Combine downbeat chords in the left hand with the pattern from Variation 29, and invent a new variation. Listen for unmusical parallels between the hands, especially the bass and the top note of the right hand. Improvise several versions with this pattern and then transpose to many other keys. Reverse the right-hand pattern so that the first note is lower than the second. Go back to the new progression you wrote and improvise this pattern over it, again transposing to several different keys.

Variation 34 provides an example of activity for the left hand. The pattern is very common throughout the eighteenth century, and does not present a complete triad but only one or two pitches. In the first measure of Variation 34, the only "real" note is G. The F♯ is a neighbor tone that serves to decorate the primary note while also providing rhythmic energy. The second measure of the variation shows a pattern with two essential notes, F♯ and D. The C♯ is the neighbor tone.

EXERCISE: Play Variation 34 and transpose it. Use your original progression and improvise something resembling Variation 34. Transpose to several keys.

In Variations 37–42 we encounter scales. Scales may "stand in" for chords if the starting and ending notes of the scales fit the chord. Our ears accept all the nonchord tones of the scale as harmonically appropriate if the scale starts and ends somewhere logical. For example, all the notes in the left hand's first measure of Variation 37 really just add up to a G.

Conveniently, a scale spanning one octave contains eight notes, which often works out favorably for rhythmic placement if we are playing in meters with duple divisions. Pieces in triple meters frequently employ clever little "bookends" to make scale passages work out rhythmically. The scale may start late, after the downbeat, or use some kind of extension to fill out the remainder of the measure.

As a side note, the fifth variation from Händel's *Harmonious Blacksmith* (E major Suite, HWV 430) uses scales in this incredibly convenient manner. Each thirty-second note scale really stands for a single melody note. See Example 6.1.

In Variation 37, the left-hand scales do not get started with sixteenths right away but rather "waste time" on an eighth note. The effect is to delay the concluding note of the scale to beat 3. In contrast with the *Harmonious*

EXAMPLE 6.1   From Händel, example of a scale representing a pitch.

Blacksmith example, which contains and completes the scale within the beat, Variation 37 pushes the arrival to the next strong beat. This strategy allows the improviser to continue the same harmony into the next beat, whereas the *Harmonious Blacksmith* approach allows the harmony to change on the following beat. If Variation 37 were in $\frac{2}{4}$ time, the left hand could play all sixteenths in a descending scale, the scale would outline an octave, and each measure would be filled. But because it is in $\frac{3}{4}$, the delay allows for an extra upward leap in eighth notes at the end of the bar, which connects nicely with the scale in the next measure. The lesson for the improviser is that basic materials such as scales must be customized—cut or expanded to fit—for every situation. It is like installing carpet or tailoring a suit.

EXERCISE: Play Variation 37 and transpose it. Play the left hand "upside down," using ascending instead of descending scales. What happens if you play all sixteenths in the scale and thus arrive "early" on the lower bass note? Find a way to fill in the remaining beats. Now use your original progression and improvise uses of the Variation 37 pattern, and do so in several different keys.

Variation 38 places the scale in the right hand, and fills in the last beat of the measure with repeated notes. Variation 39 plays off Variation 37; it is the same note-for-note except that the left-hand part has been turned upside down. Variation 40 moves the scale to the right hand. Variation 41 trades the scale between the hands, and whichever hand does not have the scale plays energetic repeated chords. Variation 42 trades scales once again, and at one point both hands play scales in tenths. After studying these variations we observe that inventing different ways of playing around with scales is not difficult at all.

EXERCISE: Improvise several variations in the manner of Variations 37–42. Use Händel's theme, and then your original theme. Transpose your improvisations to other keys.

Variations 48 and 49 create interest through rhythmic alteration. We have already learned that it is possible to improvise a variation by simple arpeggiation of the theme's harmonies. Variations 48 and 49 do so with the additional interest of dotted rhythms. It would be equally possible to use any other rhythmic idea you wish, as long as it is stylistically appropriate.

EXERCISE: Improvise several variations on Händel's theme and your own, using interesting rhythmic ideas to enliven arpeggiated figurations. Transpose to several keys.

At this point you have encountered many variation strategies. As you see, in Händel's music they consist mostly of ingenious ways of elaborating a chord progression by means of interesting keyboard textures. Thorough knowledge of the underlying progression is crucial if you are to improvise variations fluently. If these exercises have proved too difficult, it is probably because you are not sufficiently familiar with your progression. (When classical pianists begin to learn improvisation they are usually very surprised to find out just how comprehensively we need to know our progressions.)

EXERCISE: As a concluding exercise on Händel's music, choose several variation strategies from his piece and use them to improvise on your original progression. Practice them in several different keys and then perform your own chaconne, playing your theme and variations in succession.

We will consider one other variation composition in detail. Christian Friedrich Witt (c. 1660–1717) wrote a passacaglia for keyboard, which until quite recently was attributed to J. S. Bach. Witt's passacaglia in D minor is a useful collection of improvisation ideas. We will study Witt's complete piece before undertaking further exercises. The complete score appears at the end of this chapter as Example 6.3, and you should refer to it frequently while reading the following.

The theme's bass descends by step to the dominant, which is a very common pattern for passacaglias. (That is why this pattern is known as passacaglia bass.) It then repeats the move to complete the eight-measure theme. The theme consists of two 4-bar phrases which are identical except for the melodic material in the final measure and a half. This two-phrase structure will carry forward into the variations, where the second half of each variation will often alter the material from the first half—a variation upon a variation, as it were.

Note that in keeping with Witt's practice the theme is marked as 1. The first variation is marked 2. For clarity, we will retain his system.

Variation 2 is built upon a dotted rhythm, which we also observed in Händel. The right hand approximately follows the contours of the theme's melody, filling in passing tones in order to allow for the extra notes required by the dotted rhythm. The left hand provides a simple accompaniment.

Variation 3 inverts the first, placing dotted rhythms in the left hand and a sparse accompaniment in the upper voices. The downbeat of each measure in the left hand arrives on the important bass notes, with the remainder of each measure meandering around nearby neighbor and chord tones.

Variation 4 introduces a new rhythm. Significantly, the accompanying voices cover the bass and inner voice by moving in parallel tenths. Given the bass progression on which this passacaglia is built, the presence of parallel tenths is inevitable throughout the composition. The improviser benefits from this predictability because the parallel tenths are always available as a navigation aid to voice-leading; no matter what kind of variation may be in play, the tenths are always present, helping the improviser stay on track harmonically. The second half of this variation simply transposes the higher accompanying voice up one octave.

Variation 5 sends the recently introduced rhythm to the left hand. Additionally, the left-hand line augments rhythmic interest by playfully jumping back and forth between octaves.

Variation 6 changes rhythms but continues the idea of bouncing between octaves, while the sixth variation continues the same idea, but with the hands reversing roles.

EXAMPLE 6.2.1, 6.2.2, 6.2.3, 6.2.4 Excerpts from Händel's chaconne, HWV 422.

EXAMPLE 6.2.1, 6.2.2, 6.2.3, 6.2.4   Continued

EXAMPLE 6.2.1, 6.2.2, 6.2.3, 6.2.4 Continued

EXAMPLE 6.2.1, 6.2.2, 6.2.3, 6.2.4   Continued

EXAMPLE 6.3.1, 6.3.2, 6.3.3, 6.3.4, 6.3.5   Christian Friedrich Witt's passacaglia.

EXAMPLE 6.3.1, 6.3.2, 6.3.3, 6.3.4, 6.3.5 Continued

EXAMPLE 6.3.1, 6.3.2, 6.3.3, 6.3.4, 6.3.5 Continued

EXAMPLE 6.3.1, 6.3.2, 6.3.3, 6.3.4, 6.3.5 Continued

EXAMPLE 6.3.1, 6.3.2, 6.3.3, 6.3.4, 6.3.5   Continued

Variation 8 changes textures completely, presenting an alternating-hands pattern.

Variation 9 introduces constant sixteenth notes for the first time. The line is constructed around chord tones and neighbors.

Variation 10 employs a bass pattern we have observed in Händel: an octave jump with a neighbor tone, and the tenth variation consists largely of right hand descending scales. Perhaps it should be no surprise that the eleventh variation further develops this material by mixing ascending and descending scales in the left hand.

Variation 13 presents scales in both hands moving in parallel tenths, as we might have predicted, and the thirteenth variation employs the octave-leap-plus-neighbor in both hands, also in tenths.

Variation 15 fills each measure with one enormous scale in which both hand participate. As always, the first and last notes of the scale determine what chord it represents.

Variation 16 again uses tenths, but in a clever way. The scales are in canon (precise imitation) with one starting two notes before the other.

Variation 17 takes advantage of the fact that ❺ is almost consonant with all the chords within the progression, and deploys an obstinate right-hand broken octave on that note, doubling in speed for the second phrase.

Variation 18 is a fanfare in chords. What an easy idea for the improviser!

Variation 19 fills in all the melodic intervals of a fourth with stepwise sixteenth notes. We learned about this process in the chapter on diminution.

The theme appears again at the end as Variation 20 to wrap things up.

EXERCISE: Play Witt's composition and notice both the simplicity of the bass line and the wide array of variation strategies, making mental notes about your favorites.

EXERCISE: We will now work on improvising short but complete pieces in variation form. Start by choosing a chord progression from Example 6.4. It is only possible to improvise on a progression when you know it inside and out, so memorize your progression and learn to play it in several different keys. When you can play it in several keys without stopping, you are ready to improvise. Choose some variation strategies from Example 6.5, or make up your own. You may wish to write down your strategies in your zibaldone—one measure is usually long enough to remind you how each one will work—and keep them in view as you practice. Figure out how to apply the strategy to each chord within your progression. Practice your variations slowly as you figure out how to manage all the questions of rhythm, texture, and voice-leading that will inevitably arise. You should not feel that you are cheating if you work out most of your variation in some detail before playing straight through. Your goal is to play your theme followed by three variations. Again, you may need to plan and practice your variations almost to the point of memorizing them like a script. Don't worry; mastery must come first; spontaneity comes later. Once you are comfortable with your piece, keep the same theme and variation strategies, but transpose them to other keys. Keep playing your piece in several keys until you are good at it.

The possibility for improvising variations on a theme is seemingly endless. At the same time, long sets of variations can be tiresome. After all, it is not musically interesting to hear every imaginable elaboration and permutation of one chord progression. Händel demonstrated a way to break up this repetition.

EXAMPLE 6.4.1 AND 6.4.2   Sample chord progressions for variations.

Witt: Passacaglia in D minor. The "standard" Passacaglia progression.

Händel: Chaconne in G, HWV 435 (simplified). The "Goldberg" progression.

Händel: Chaconne in G, HWV 435, minor section (simplified). Four bars of Passacaglia, and four of RO.

Händel: Passacaglia in G minor, HWV 432.

Händel: Chaconne in C, HWV 443. The "Monte Romanesca" or ascending fifths progression (half of a C5, played backwards).

Rameau: Gavotte with Six Doubles (first part of Gavotte).

EXAMPLE 6.4.1 AND 6.4.2 Continued

Jean-Nicholas Geoffroy:
Chaconne in E major

JCF Fischer: Chaconne in F major

Pasquini: Passacaglia

Anonymous: La Folia

His chaconne in G major (HWV 435)—not the one we just studied—provides contrast by moving to the parallel key for a few variations.

The first issue to consider when planning a contrasting section in a parallel key is how your chords will work when harmonically modified. Generally speaking, chord progressions in major keys can be converted to minor, but the improviser must be aware of any necessary adaptations, which usually have to do with the chromatic alterations of the sixth and (especially) seventh scale degrees in minor. Händel used a substantially different progression in the parallel key area within the chaconne mentioned earlier. A simplified version of the minor progression from HWV 435 appears in Example 6.4.

EXAMPLE 6.5.1 AND 6.5.2   Examples of variation strategies.

EXERCISE: Take a chord progression on which you have already improvised variations. Move it to the parallel key and figure out how the chords must be altered. Again, choose three or more variation strategies and work them out over the new progression. As always, transpose and play until you are good at it.

EXAMPLE 6.5.1 AND 6.5.2 Continued

EXERCISE: This exercise is quite ambitious. Combine the major and minor versions of your progression. Use one version as the opening section with three or more variations, the parallel key area as a middle section with three or more variations, and the first version once again, with yet three more variations, to conclude. Though this exercise is very challenging, you already have the knowledge to do it, if you proceed patiently and master every step before going on. When you can play your piece confidently, perform it in front of others.

EXERCISE: As a final exercise, use a progression that is very familiar, and do not plan your variations in advance. Instead, keep your book open to the table of strategies, and choose them "in the moment" as you are playing. Alternatively, use your own set of variation strategies from your zibaldone. Keep your tempo slow, and try to stay in time and play without stopping.

You now know enough about variations to improvise at greater length. To work on variations further, try more of the progressions in Example 6.4, or create your own. In your zibaldone, create a collection of variation strategies and useful chord progressions for this improvisation technique.

Chapter 7

Lyricism

In this chapter we will learn to improvise pieces in a lyrical style, with particular attention to the following qualities:

1. A slow tempo.
2. The soprano voice serving in the most prominent role, displaying elaborate ornamentation and an expressive lyrical character.
3. An accompaniment (bass and inner voices) employing consistent rhythmic and textural patterns that, while attractive and expressive in their own right, support the primacy of the soprano. The accompaniment may feature persistent pulsation, not aggressive or anxious, but more like a heartbeat or breathing, imbuing pieces in this style with a sense of sincerity and earnestness.

Slow pieces with these qualities may appear as middle movements of concerti, suite movements, a prelude to another work, or may stand alone. The style is flexible and appropriate for many occasions, and lends itself to improvisation because a slow tempo allows more time for planning and foresight in the midst of performance.

We will start by improvising over a given chord progression. While experienced improvisers could certainly invent a chord progression on the fly, for now we will use an existing chord pattern so that we may give all our attention to creating melody. The opening movement of J. C. F. Fischer's suite in D minor ("Uranie") will serve as our harmonic template. Example 7.1 displays the piece in its entirety. (Note that Fischer calls it a toccata. Clearly, musicians of the eighteenth century did not necessarily think all toccatas had to be fast and virtuosic.)

Example 7.2 shows a simplified version of the first two measures of the Fischer, followed by a realization for the left hand alone, and finally the same thing in consistent pulsing eighth notes. The harmonic progression is very

EXAMPLE 7.1   J. C. F. Fischer's toccata in D minor from "Uranie" Suite.

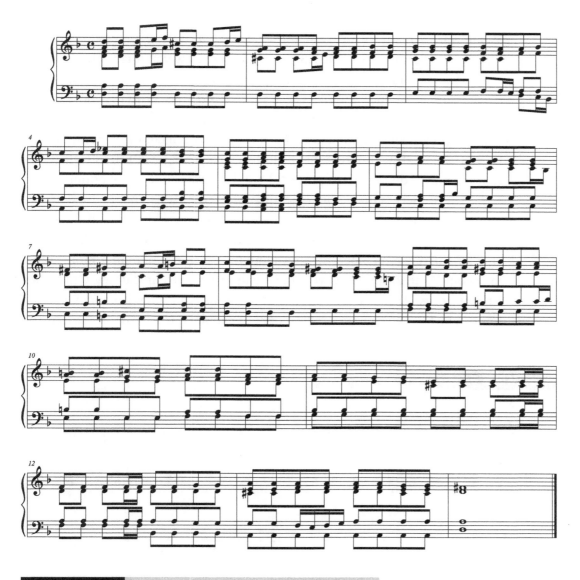

EXAMPLE 7.2   Accompaniment pattern for improvisation.

simple: tonic and dominant over a ① pedal in the bass. By creating a version for
the left hand alone, we free the right hand to improvise melody.

EXERCISE: Play measures 3 and 4 of Example 7.2. As you loop around
and play these four chords repeatedly, improvise a simple melody in the right

hand. Start by using only chord tones in simple rhythms such as quarter notes. As you become more confident, begin to use eighth notes, adding passing tones, rhythmic inflections, and anything else that seems interesting and appropriate. When you are ready, switch from the left-hand half-note accompaniment to the eighth-note version. Example 7.3 shows one idea how you might proceed.

Clearly, your improvised melody must match and affirm the harmonic progression. That does not mean that notes outside the chord may not be used; they certainly can. But they must conform to the eighteenth-century rules regarding treatment of dissonances (also known as nonchord or nonharmonic tones). The treatment of dissonance in this style is very careful. In eighteenth-century music, dissonance is powerful but dangerous, like a love potion.

Any undergraduate theory course will cover this matter in detail. If you never took theory (or slept through it), you should review the types of dissonances and procedures for handing them before you go further in this chapter. I barely remember learning about the categories of nonharmonic tones in school. At that time they were merely inscrutable technicalities. Only when I began to use them in the creation of real music did they become vivid and important to me. Your improvisational vocabulary will grow in variety and

EXAMPLE 7.3   Examples of improvised lines.

EXAMPLE 7.4   Adding dissonances to a melody.

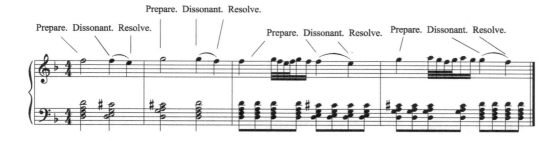

richness if you study and master suspensions, passing and neighbor tones, appoggiaturas, and all other nonharmonic tones.

The tasteful and discerning use of dissonance can create moments of re-markable beauty in a melody. Because many dissonances are prepared by common tone and resolved by step, an obvious place to use them is at the mo-ment of a chord change. In that case, we look for a note that fits the first chord but not the second chord. It can sing merrily along with the first chord, but when the harmony shifts underneath it, suddenly it is dissonant, like a cartoon character running straight off a cliff and realizing that there is no ground be-neath him. When he looks around and realizes his predicament, he falls.

A note that occurs only in the i chord but not in V⁷ is ❸. Likewise, ❹ occurs in V⁷ but not in i. We can use these scale degrees to create dissonances over our chord progression. Example 7.4 shows a simple use of these dissonances, followed by a more elaborate realization. Note that two instances of dissonance/resolution in corresponding locations make for an attractive phrase structure.

EXERCISE: Improvise melodies over the two bars we have already used from Example 7.3. Find all the scale degrees that can be prepared over the i chord but are dissonant over the V⁷, and vice versa, and use each in an impro-vised phrase. Begin with very simple melodies, playing only the notes required for preparation, dissonance, and resolution. After that, embellish your tunes with techniques such as turns and passing tones.

We will now use more of Fischer's progression. Example 7.5 shows the entire piece in a reduced left-hand accompaniment. (A few of the chords have been altered to accommodate small hands, and some of the voice-leading cheats for the same reason.) Beneath the bass staff, figures indicate harmony. These are the harmonies you need to think about as you improvise melodic material over each chord.

EXERCISE: Using Example 7.5, improvise a melody while playing the left-hand part as written. Start with long values only (quarter and half notes) using chord tones only. In constructing your melody, try to avoid duplicating the notes in the bass line too often, as this would produce noticeable and ob-jectionable parallels. Repeat the exercise many times, gradually adding eighth

EXAMPLE 7.5 Fischer's toccata as a left-hand accompaniment.

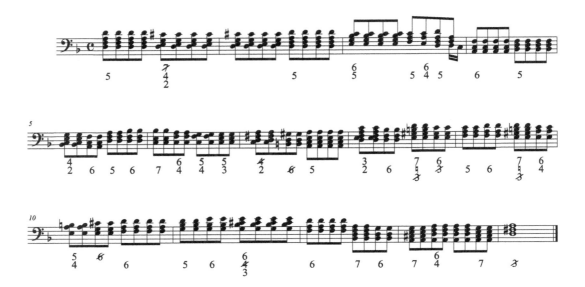

notes, passing and neighbor tones, suspensions, and any other elements that are stylistically appropriate and do not disturb your even, steady rhythm, or sabotage your concentration.

Eighteenth-century musicians considered elaborate decoration to be tasteful and expressive. (One may make comparisons with eighteenth-century architecture, interior design, and horticulture.) In the lyrical approach, elaboration takes place primarily in the soprano voice. The manner of elaboration is variegated, exulting in seemingly endless ways of approaching, decorating, and moving from structural chord tones. Therefore, the improviser's methods of decoration must change constantly. We may gain facility in playing highly elaborated soprano lines if we study systematically the kinds of decoration typical of the style.

One way to begin developing an elaboration strategy is to deploy diminutions, as we have studied previously. However, ordinary diminutions will sound too uniform for this style, and will require modification. Example 7.6 shows a simple voice-leading outline of a passage, a version of the same thing with diminutions applied, and another version showing variegation of those diminutions. The third version is the original piece as composed by Johann Ludwig Krebs (1713–1780), the prelude from the partita in B♭.

Notice how many different methods Krebs uses to connect the underlying structural tones in the soprano. The "plain" diminutions in the second version connect all the notes as well, but in a uniform manner. Generally, uniform diminutions are for fast tempi and variegated elaborations are for slow tempi. We can organize these elaborations into three broad categories: stepwise, leaps, and stationary.

Stepwise elaborations include any motion by step, whether a simple half step or a large scale of an octave or more. Leaps will usually involve arpeggiation

EXAMPLE 7.6   Three versions of Krebs' Prelude.

of a specific harmony. Stationary elaborations are ornaments that decorate a note without moving it to another note. Example 7.7 shows three instances of elaborations selected from Marcello, Krebs, and Bach. Study these passages and note the variety each composer employs.

We may create lyrical elaborations by identifying structural melody notes and then connecting them with various techniques. For each chord in the accompaniment, the improviser should choose a chord tone from which to begin. If the duration of the chord is long, one may connect the first chord tone with another from the same harmony, using stepwise or leaping motion and variegated rhythm. One may also create a stationary ornament and stay on the same chord tone. As the next chord change approaches, the improviser must choose a chord tone from this new harmony and travel to it by means of another elaboration.

The middle movement of Bach's Italian Concerto may serve as a catalog of examples of elaborations in the lyrical style. You may wish to play through it at the piano and write down some of his techniques in your zibaldone. Note how long his phrases are. How does he keep the melody going for so long? What devices does he use to maintain (and eventually release) dramatic tension?

EXERCISE: Example 7.8 shows a voice-leading outline in the right hand with a chordal accompaniment in the left. The notes in the right hand serve as target notes. Play through the example as written. Then try various strategies to connect each written note with the next one. Use stepwise motion in various rhythms, leaps, and stationary ornaments. Transpose the exercise to other keys. Further on in Example 7.8, two possible solutions appear.

EXAMPLE 7.7   Examples from Marcello, Krebs, and Bach.

Now that you have worked on connecting given structural notes, the next step is to create your own. A melody should have an interesting overall shape. While many different shapes are possible, a gradually rising line is usually a reliable choice as it provides a sense of forward motion and drama.

EXERCISE: Using the progression from Example 7.9, map out the structural melody notes for a gradually rising line. You should reach the highest

EXAMPLE 7.8 Simple piece with examples of elaboration.

EXAMPLE 7.9 Accompaniment pattern for improvisation practice.

point shortly before the end, but save a little time to descend before the conclusion. You may also wish to note which chord could support the moment of greatest melodic interest and intensity. Once you have created a structural melody, try out various ways to elaborate it. Use stepwise, leaping, and stationary techniques and a wide variety of rhythms and patterns. Suspend tones over harmonic changes to create interesting moments of dissonance. Transpose and try it in other keys.

So far we have only used accompaniments of repeating eighth notes. While the left hand is not the focus of this style, we do have more options. The pizzicato bass accompaniment appears in the D major Orchestral Suite of J. S. Bach as well as the slow movement of his F minor Keyboard Concerto. The same composer's G minor Keyboard Concerto uses a striking pattern in the bass during ritornello sections of the slow movement. Between extended statements by the soloist, the orchestra chimes in with a refrain characterized by an interesting rhythm. Improvising soloists may borrow all these ideas, which are set forth in Example 7.10.

EXERCISE: Example 7.11 provides six measures from the J. S. Bach D major orchestral suite with a pizzicato bass. Use scores or recordings to figure out what chords Bach used above the bass. If necessary, copy the bass into your zibaldone and use figured bass symbols, Roman analysis, noted chords in the treble staff, or modern chord symbols (whichever helps you most). Then compose a few melodies in structural notes only. Practice connecting the structural notes with elaborations as discussed above. Then try inventing your structural notes on the fly, without notation. As a further challenge, invent both

EXAMPLE 7.10 Bass line ideas.

EXAMPLE 7.11 Example of pizzicato bass.

the structural notes and connecting elaborations without any use of notation. Finally, transpose the entire exercise into other keys.

EXERCISE: Invent a four-measure chord progression in common time with harmonies that changes on beats 1 and 3 of every measure. Use the pizzicato bass from the Bach F minor Concerto as a left-hand accompaniment. First play your piece with right-hand chords and left-hand pizzicato. Then improvise elaborations in the right hand while the left hand plays the pizzicato pattern. Transpose to other keys. Revisit your progression using the other accompaniments from Example 7.10.

In your zibaldone, develop a collection of lyrical ornamentation techniques, categorized by whether they cover unisons, steps, or leaps.

Chapter 8

Suite

Friedrich Erhard Niedt (1674–1717) wrote his *Musicalische Handleitung* (*Musical Guide*) in the first decade of the 1700s. He devoted one chapter to instruction on using a short figured bass as a starting point for improvising dance suite movements. Niedt recommended learning a single bass pattern and its harmony very thoroughly, and then customizing the rhythm and stylistic elements to create the various dance pieces of that time such as allemandes, courantes, sarabandes, and gigues.

In this chapter we will follow Niedt's advice. We will begin with the bass line he recommends, and then learn to overlay the appropriate harmonies in block chords. After that, we will accommodate our chord progression to the various rhythmic requirements of each dance. Finally, we will use techniques of diminution to elaborate the progression and make it sound like real music. Our goal is to improvise complete dance suites in a variety of keys.

Example 8.1 depicts Niedt's bass:

EXERCISE: Memorize the bass line in C major. Note that it follows the form of a bipartite dance in a major key, in which the first part (A) begins on I and concludes by tonicizing V, and the second (B) begins on V and concludes with a cadence on I. In performance, the sections are repeated. Next, work out the upper voices in block chords (if you need help, see Example 8.2). Note that the opening gesture is our old friend the Page One progression. Keep the voice-leading sensible and melodic, especially in the soprano voice. The soprano may begin in any position of the first chord. Learn multiple positions of the upper voices so that you can vary them at will. When you are confident in C major, practice it in other major keys until you are fluent. Practice the progression in rhythm, using a metronome.

This progression may serve as the harmonic structure for any short bipartite piece, but we will learn four of the most common dances that comprise the suite: allemande, courante, sarabande, and gigue. The allemande is in $\frac{4}{4}$ at

EXAMPLE 8.1 The Niedt bass.

EXAMPLE 8.2 The Niedt bass with chords.

a moderate tempo. It always begins each section with an anacrusis, either a single eighth or sixteenth pickup, or a group of three sixteenths immediately before the downbeat. The courante is in moderate or quick triple meter but its subdivisions are usually duple. An example would be $\frac{3}{4}$ with running sixteenths or $\frac{3}{2}$ with running eighths. Like the allemande, it will likely have an anacrusis. The sarabande is a gracious piece in slow $\frac{3}{4}$. The soprano will be featured as a lyrical, ornamented melody. Lilting rhythms will appear throughout. The gigue is a fast compound meter piece in $\frac{6}{8}$ or $\frac{9}{8}$ (sometimes $\frac{12}{8}$) and may use running triplets, quarter-eighth patterns, or dotted triplets.

Although Example 8.2 shows Niedt's progression in four voices, we have no obligation to keep all four sounding all the time. In the Great Suites of Händel (HWV426–433), the French Suites of Bach (BWV 812–817), and the *Musicalisher Parnassus* of J. C. F. Fischer (as well as countless other examples), the polyphonic texture changes freely from two voices up to five or more within a single movement. Three seems to be the average. While homophonic textures do occur, the norm is to "activate" every voice with attention-grabbing independent rhythmic motion just often enough to maintain a sense of polyphony. However, the shortest note values (often sixteenths) usually occur in just one voice at a time, with limited instances of parallel motion in the fastest note values. Generally, a texture with fewer voices allows each to be more active rhythmically. You need not generate an absolutely constant, seamless flow of notes. Dance suite movements "breathe" a little bit more than some other eighteenth-century pieces; stopping here and there on a few longer chords is within the stylistic boundaries of this music.

All this is good news for the improviser. We do not need to keep track of a strict number of voices; rather, we can expand and contract the texture at will, even changing suddenly from a sparse two-voice passage to very full chords. Nor do we need to keep every voice in frenetic rhythmic activity on every beat.

Now that we know this figured bass progression thoroughly, we can start to make music with it by adding diminutions to create an allemande. You may wish to review the table of diminutions from the appropriate chapter. You should plan on memorizing them as soon as possible.

EXERCISE: Using the realization of Niedt's bass in Example 8.2, play through the progression and embellish the soprano with diminutions. Any quarter note may transform into four sixteenths; the first sixteenth should be the pitch of the written quarter note, and the following three should form a diminution that connects to the next beat. Do not feel obligated to maintain the full four-voice texture when adding diminutions, as this is generally impossible, but do try to keep the harmonies complete. When you encounter a half note, you may treat it as two quarter notes of the same pitch. For longer chords at the end of the A and B sections, it is not desirable to fill in all the beats with diminutions, as these moments should communicate a sense of repose. After playing through the example several times with soprano diminutions, move the diminutions to another voice. Then go through yet again and trade diminutions between voices. After this, allow yourself the freedom not to fill in every beat with four sixteenths; vary the rhythmic texture and trade diminutions between the voices, imitating the style you observe in the eighteenth-century dance suite repertoire. You will probably make voice-leading errors when you start adding diminutions; parallel fifths and octaves may occur accidentally. This is a normal problem. When it happens, take note of why, and try to find a different solution. Finally, repeat this whole process transposed to several other keys. Do not go on to greater levels of difficulty until you have completely mastered the task at hand.

The final step in creating an allemande is to incorporate the anacrusis. The simplest version is a single eighth or sixteenth note on one of the tones of the first chord. Most allemandes of Bach begin this way.

However, with an anacrusis consisting of three stepwise sixteenths, you may then incorporate that same figure throughout your improvisation in order to create satisfying thematic unity. The B minor allemande from the French Suites does this. A good strategy is to construct the anacrusis out of the last three notes of a diminution that will be easy to deploy repeatedly throughout the piece. Example 8.3 depicts an anacrusis that matches nicely with some of the diminutions.

EXERCISE: Improvise an allemande using the techniques from the previous exercise, but add an anacrusis before each reprise. Work on keeping sixteenth notes flowing much of the time, until the end of each reprise when you can rest on the concluding chord. Try improvising allemandes in several different major keys. At first, you might wish to keep the chord realization (Example 8.2) in front of you, but try playing the progression from memory when you are able. Use a metronome at a very slow tempo. When you practice, you should not feel like you are solving problems in desperation at the absolute last moment, but rather that you have plenty of time to think. Slow down your metronome if your playing is not serene and confident.

We have started to improvise by adding diminutions to a chord progression, dropping notes from the texture as needed to make room for the diminutions. An alternative approach is to use compound melody in the right hand, keeping the given bass. As you will recall from the diminution chapter, compound

EXAMPLE 8.3   Example of allemande anacrusis.

EXAMPLE 8.4 Compound melody in a Händel allemande.

melody is a single line of constantly running notes that implies a thicker polyphonic texture by leaping between registers. A compound melody is like a ventriloquist act in which one person creates the illusion of conversation by rapidly alternating between the voices of the performer and the dummy. Example 8.4, from the allemande of Händel's suite HWV 438, shows the composer's original followed by a chordal simplification. Both hands employ compound melody. In each hand it creates two or three lines out of one, and includes a neighbor tone in the right hand's lower voice, as well.

The difference between these two ways of improvising is that the first starts with the intact, four-voice progression, but leaves out voices as required by the activity of the diminutions. The second does not concern itself with keeping all the voices present, but merely implies their existence from time to time. Each approach is legitimate and effective, and real music includes both techniques. To develop your ability to improvise compound melody, we will return once again to Niedt's figured bass as realized in Example 8.2.

EXERCISE: Play the chord progression by keeping the bass as written in the left hand but creating a right hand consisting of running sixteenths that outline each harmony. Use only a single line (i.e., one note at a time; no chords), but try to outline the important chord factors in each harmony. At first, use only chord tones. When you succeed at this, add nonharmonic tones to your line. The easiest and most fool-proof nonharmonic tones are the passing tones that fill in chord tones a third apart. These will almost always sound good. Neighboring tones are generally safe, as well. Add others as you become more confident. Example 8.5 provides possible solutions.

Example 8.6 shows the first four measures of the realized chord progression followed by a possible solution in compound melody, including nonchord tones. Once you are comfortable realizing the progression with compound melody, transpose to several other keys.

Rhythmic Activation

The essence of polyphonic music is independence of line; each voice must sound alive and interesting. When improvising in a three- or four-voice texture, attending to the well-being of all the voices may seem like a harrowing task, like

EXAMPLE 8.5   Solution for single-line melody, without and with nonchord tones.

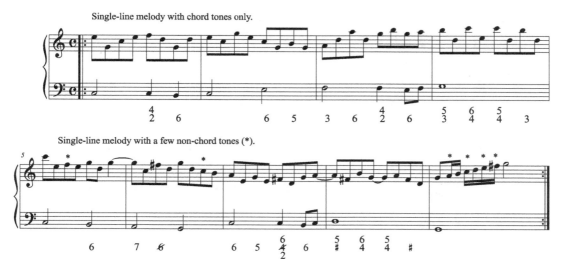

EXAMPLE 8.6   Compound melody realization of the Niedt bass.

keeping track of the flight path of every honeybee in a swarm. One way to maintain a lively sense of polyphony without overwhelming your intellect is to use rhythmic activation, or restriking notes near the end of their duration (typically resulting in a dotted rhythm of some kind). You encountered this concept in the diminution chapter. The restruck note gives that voice a hint of individuality as well as momentum, as it acts as a forward-leaning anacrusis. Its effect is more pronounced if the short note is staccato.

Example 8.7 shows the opening measures of Niedt's progression, followed by a version with rhythmic activations. Note that we have not added any new pitches to the original chord progression, yet now it sounds more polyphonic—that is, more layered and interesting. The technique of rhythmic activation is

EXAMPLE 8.7   Rhythmic activation of the Niedt bass.

especially useful whenever the improviser needs to enliven the texture but may not have time to prepare diminutions.

A specific use of rhythmic activation appears very often in the suites of Bach, Händel, Fischer, and many others. On the downbeat of the piece the bass usually plays ①. Immediately thereafter a tenor voice appears and presents an anacrusis and arrival on the second beat. These two notes could be any two factors of the tonic chord, but most likely will be ❺ ascending to ❶. Since we like to name things, let us call this kind of rhythmic activation the *Me Too*. It is as if the tenor is late to the party, not having arrived on the downbeat, and wishes to assert its participation in the fun. Examples 8.8, 8.9, and 8.10 show instances of the Me Too taken from Bach and Händel.

For the improviser, the advantage of the Me Too is that it merely fills in notes from a chord we already know, and so does not require extra harmonic thinking. At the same time, it implies the entrance of new voices in a satisfying polyphonic manner. Further, it contrasts effectively with faster-moving note values which may be in the right hand. Finally, the Me Too is a strong stylistic gesture that contributes to the historical legitimacy of an improvisation. It may be used in any voice (not necessarily the tenor) at any point in an improvisation whenever you wish to fill out a particular harmony without committing to complex diminutions.

EXERCISE: To practice rhythmic activation and the Me Too, we return to the realization of Niedt's bass as shown in Example 8.2. Play the progression as written, but activate one of the voices of each chord by using either a rhythmic activation or a Me Too. Play through several times, varying your activations among the voices in diverse and creative ways. As always, try this in several keys.

The majority of eighteenth-century allemandes proceed in more or less constant sixteenth notes, with voices taking turns providing rhythmic activity.

EXAMPLE 8.8 Example of "Me Too."

EXAMPLE 8.9 Example of "Me Too."

EXAMPLE 8.10 Example of "Me Too."

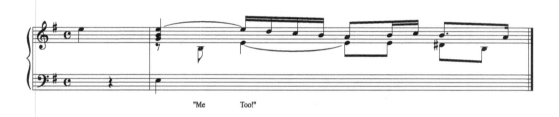

However, once in a while we encounter some interesting rhythmic variations within the allemande style. J. C. F. Fischer used a quick thirty-second-note diminution in his *Clio* and *Melpomene* allemandes, as did Bach in the F major English Suite. Bach follows the thirty-second notes with sixteenth note triplets. John Loeillet provides us with an allemande in dotted rhythms. See Example 8.11.

These diminutions and triplets are easy to add to your texture if you use them to fill in between chord tones. Triplets fit beautifully within any triad, of course: one merely travels between the root and third or third and fifth in either direction. If the chord has a seventh, one can fill in the space between fifth and seventh. The thirty-second notes must be given more care: if you copy *Clio* and repeat the first thirty-second, the diminution will span a fourth. If you copy *Melpomene* and don't repeat notes, the diminution will span a fifth. The point is that you need to think ahead so that your diminution lands on a chord tone.

Unlike inventions, fugues, and many other keyboard pieces of the eighteenth century, allemandes may not display motivic unity. Economic and pervasive use of tight, recognizable motives appears not to have been a priority of

EXAMPLE 8.11   Rhythmic variety within the allemande style.

EXAMPLE 8.12   Motivic unity in allemandes.

most composers of allemandes. It is stylistically fitting, therefore, to improvise allemandes without worrying about using repeating motivic material.

On the other hand, allemandes with no unity may seem a bit homogenous and even forgettable. A manageable strategy for creating a modicum of unity is to start each section of the bipartite form with similar melodic and rhythmic gestures. While this method does not imbue the improvisation with comprehensive motivic unity, it does present just enough similarity between the beginnings of the sections such that the piece sounds more purposeful. Example 8.12 shows beginnings of A and B sections which are motivically unified.

Initially, even the simplest improvisation on the Niedt progression will take up all your mental powers. However, as you gradually gain facility, you may wish to inform your dance suite improvisations with motivic unity by starting the A and B sections with similar rhythmic and intervallic material.

Courante

Like the allemande, the courante is typically in moderate or fast tempo, starts each section with an anacrusis, and is mostly filled in with consistently running notes that may jump freely between voices. Improvising the courante will call upon all the same skills as the allemande, but now adapted to a new meter. While courantes may appear in any triple meter with duple subdivisions, Niedt chooses $\frac{6}{4}$. Example 8.13 shows how he alters his bass to fit the metrical requirements of the courante.

EXERCISE: Begin by making your own chordal realization of Niedt's courante bass. You may write it out, but the challenge and benefit will be greater if you do it at sight. Play your realization as musically as possible, and stay in $\frac{6}{4}$ time. Once you are fluent in the chordal realization, apply all the exercises we used while learning the allemande. Embellish the soprano with diminutions in eighth notes, noting that chords with the duration of one quarter note can only take two eighths as a diminution. Play through several more times, each time choosing a different voice to embellish. Then trade freely between voices. Return to the simple chordal realization, and play through it adding rhythmic activations and Me Too embellishments to various voices. Add a single-note anacrusis to the beginning of each reprise. Next, go through the progression once again, this time preserving the bass line and generating right-hand material by means of compound melody. As a last step, freely mix all these techniques in your improvisations, and transpose to several other keys.

A courante in $\frac{6}{4}$ with running eighth notes is quite a different animal from one in $\frac{3}{4}$ with running sixteenths. Each has twelve of the smallest values per measure, but their metrical organization is not the same. The former has

EXAMPLE 8.13   The Niedt bass as a courante.

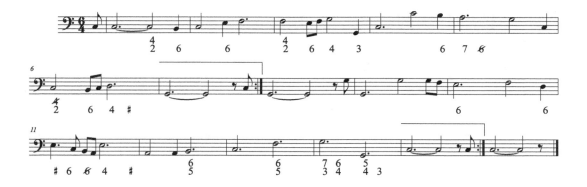

two groups of six, further divided into three groups of two, whereas the latter consists of three groups of four. You could certainly learn to improvise these (and other) variants of suite movements, but be aware that it will require the same level of work as learning a completely new type of dance. The same is true for switching between gigues in 6/8 and 9/8, to give just one example. I sometimes revert accidentally to 4/4 time if I do not give sufficient attention to the feel of the compound meter; you might have the same problem!

Sarabande

Sarabandes are fun to improvise. Due to the slower tempo, the performer has more leisure to indulge the melodic imagination and may experience less mental urgency concerning the harmonic progression. The sarabande is in 3/4, often characterized by a dotted rhythm. The style of this piece does not require constant running notes, so the performer may feel free to use very simple textures, even playing some phrases in unadorned quarter-note chords. Of course, some rhythmic variegation will provide contrast. Interestingly, Niedt insists that each section must have exactly eight measures, although this practice was not routinely observed by eighteenth-century composers. Niedt's template for the sarabande appears in Example 8.14.

EXERCISE: Improvise sarabandes. If your pieces sound boring and perfunctory, try incorporating nonharmonic tones. You can create a suspension in an upper voice over any harmonic change as long as you prepare by common tone and resolve by step. The tasteful deployment of a few suspensions (not too many!) unifies your improvisation. A unified piece of music "sounds like itself," as one of my friends likes to say. Example 8.15, showing the opening few bars, demonstrates a few instances of suspensions.

Gigue

The gigue is a lively crowd-pleaser and most often appears as the concluding movement of the suite. Unlike other suite movements, the gigue sometime serves as a template for a complex contrapuntal work, with the A section

EXAMPLE 8.14 The Niedt bass as a sarabande.

EXAMPLE 8.15   Example of suspensions in a sarabande.

EXAMPLE 8.16   The Niedt bass as a gigue.

fashioned as a fugue and the B section a second fugue, with the B section's subject derived from the A section theme played upside down.

Not all imitative gigues proceed with a complete fugue, however. Many gigues begin with a point of imitation (possibly at the fifth but more frequently at the octave) but then break off strict counterpoint. We will address issues of imitation later. For now, we will learn to play the gigue in a simpler style, which seems to have been somewhat more common than the fugal style.

Example 8.16 shows how Niedt once again adapts his bass line for a new meter.

EXERCISE: We will repeat the procedures from the previous movements as we learn the gigue. Begin by learning the bass and harmony in block chords, conforming to the meter of the gigue. Gradually introduce diminutions and compound melody in various voices, and transpose to other keys.

As mentioned, gigues vary tremendously in their levels of complexity and ambition. Some take advantage of the fact that triple meter matches nicely with triadic harmony, and employ extensive arpeggiation of triads or stepwise figures that outline thirds. In such instances you may wonder whether you are playing little more than a lightly embellished chord progression. So what? It still

EXAMPLE 8.17 Examples of gigue textures.

sounds like good music. Enjoy it. Example 8.17 shows instances of easy gigue textures. Using easy textures is the best way to start improvising gigues.

Our next step is to convert the Niedt progression to minor keys. Niedt did not provide a minor version so we will need to create our own. Obviously you can make one up (and I hope you will at some point). Example 8.18 shows one I made which begins by following Niedt but then goes off in a different direction. Note that this example modulates to the minor dominant, rather than the relative major, at the conclusion of the A section.

At this point you must start over again with all the same procedures you already used for learning suites in major keys, but now applied to the minor mode. I suggest spreading this task out over a long period of time and practicing just a few minor keys per day until you are confident in every tonality. When I first decided to learn the Niedt progression in every key, it took about three days, practicing obsessively several hours each day, until I obtained fluency with all 24 keys. By "fluency" I mean the ability to play the progression in any of the suite meters, at a moderate tempo without hesitation, varying the textures and positions of the chords at will. In other words, you should not aim to have one specific note-for-note way to play the Niedt progressions, but rather a flexible template which you can morph as you wish, in real time.

To pursue even greater mastery in improvising suites, you can create your own harmonic progressions to use in place of Niedt's. You could also add other kinds of suite movements, putting together a more elaborate suite beginning with a prelude or toccata, using techniques from the appropriate chapters. You could investigate the gavotte, minuet, or other movements we have not discussed here. Another possibility is to play doubles (just another name for variations) on a movement. One or more doubles often appeared after gavottes

EXAMPLE 8.18   A suggested version of the Niedt bass in minor.

and minuets. To improvise doubles, simply follow the procedures from the chapter on variations, using the movement in question as your harmonic basis.

Taking things a step further, it is not necessary to base all the movements of your suite on the same progression. If you learn a whole library of chord patterns, you will be able to improvise suites of satisfying variety.

Learning to improvise dance suites in the eighteenth-century style is, initially, a steep climb. However, once you gain fluency with the Niedt progression, you can improvise at length, creating several contrasting pieces based on the same chord pattern. Do not worry that listeners will notice the repeated harmonic material and call you a cheater. The contrasting rhythms and surface textures of the various pieces obscure the underlying progression to the point that even professional musicians will not notice unless someone points it out in advance. I do this in concert all the time and have never been caught. (Although now that I've admitted it in writing . . .)

In your zibaldone, develop a collection of progressions in bipartite form that you can use for suite improvisation.

Chapter 9

Imitation

Imitation is a technique in which a tune starts in one voice sounding alone, and then appears in other voices as they enter in succession. These short instances of imitative entries are called *points of imitation.*

Imitation is a defining characteristic of eighteenth-century music. Pieces not rigorously contrapuntal in construction may nevertheless begin with points of imitation, as though it were necessary to pay tribute to the tradition of imitation before proceeding with other business.

Some readers may suppose that improvising imitation is extraordinarily difficult because of its time-shifting nature. A melodic event in one voice must recur moments later in another, but meanwhile the first voice must carry on. This management of melodic material in multiple, nonsynchronous "time-lines" may seem bewildering. However, with systematic practice, simple points of imitation need not be so daunting.

In this chapter we will study techniques of improvising points of imitation. We will then learn to incorporate them into some already familiar forms such as the gigue. For purposes of this chapter, we will refer to the leading voice as the *theme*, and the second voice as the *answer.*

Imitation can occur at various intervals, meaning that the answer may not enter at the same pitch as the theme, but may be "off" by a fifth, fourth, or other interval. However, in this chapter we will only study imitation at the octave, which is when the answer starts on the same pitch (although generally in a different octave) as the theme.

The first technique of imitation is the *Play & Rest*. It avoids the problem of simultaneous, overlapping voices by including rests in the second half of the theme. The rests in the theme correspond with the entry of the answer. Example 9.1 depicts the opening of a gigue by Händel. Notice that the right hand is doing nothing when the left hand enters except for the one instant where they overlap. The Play & Rest is not common in real music, but is a useful introductory exercise.

EXAMPLE 9.1   Point of imitation from a Händel gigue.

EXAMPLE 9.2   Themes for imitation practice.

EXERCISE: Example 9.2 provides eight short themes. At the locations marked X, the answer should enter with identical material, transposed one or two octaves from the theme as appropriate. Note that some themes fill half a measure with notes and half with rests. In these cases, both the theme and its answer will fit within one measure (plus the downbeat of the following measure). The longer themes, with a full measure of notes and a full measure of rest, will require the answer to start in the second measure. Practice providing each them with an answer. Stay in tempo and play musically. Transpose these exercises to many other keys. Take all the right-hand themes and start them in the left hand, and vice-versa.

While these Play & Rest exercises are fairly simple, not just any tune will do. The theme must conclude on a note that is consonant with its beginning note. In Example 9.2, all the themes begin on ❶ and conclude on either ❶ or ❸.

This guarantees that the moment of hand-off will be harmonically stable. Further, the theme must fit logically within its meter. In $\frac{4}{4}$ time the theme may take up (for example) two or four beats. The answer will then take up the same amount, result in a complete event of one or two full measures. However, in $\frac{9}{8}$ time, we cannot use a theme of six beats, since the answer would occur on beat seven and last until beat four of the following measure. A confusing hemiola would result, causing the improviser to lose track of the meter. Therefore, in $\frac{9}{8}$, the theme must last for a full measure at minimum.

EXERCISE: Invent several themes for Play & Rest imitation. If necessary, write them down in your zibaldone. Use a variety of meters and keys. Each should be simple, memorable, and contained within the home key. Make sure the first and last notes are consonant with each other so that your hand-off makes harmonic sense. Transpose each to a wide variety of keys. Trade them between the hands.

The next imitative technique, *Play & Hold*, involves only a slight increase in complexity over Play & Rest. Instead of resting in the second half of the theme, we will hold onto a single pitch in the first voice as the answer enters. The first three bars of Example 9.3 show an instance of Play & Hold wherein the theme contains only pitches of the tonic harmony and ends on sustained ❶, ensuring harmonious agreement with the answer. In the final three bars we add an anacrusis to the theme, so now the theme and answer overlap by two notes instead of one. This kind of short overlap is quite common in simpler gigues of the eighteenth century.

In the Play & Hold technique, the held note should be ❶ for now. ❶ is consonant with tonic harmony and unlikely to clash with the answer, as long as the theme stays very close to the I chord. It is possible, of course, to add passing and neighboring tones to the theme without changing the essential harmony. However, for now they should be very simple, brief, and placed on weak beats.

EXERCISE: Example 9.4 provides three themes suitable for Play & Hold. Figure out how to provide an answer for each one. Try them in various high and low registers. Switch between the hands and transpose. Invent several of your own themes with answers.

In the next level of imitation the theme will remain active after the answer enters. The section of the first voice that overlaps with the answer we will call the *continuation*. We will call this technique *Play & Continue*. Initially we will

EXAMPLE 9.3   The Play & Hold technique.

EXAMPLE 9.4 Themes for Play & Hold practice.

EXAMPLE 9.5 The Play & Continue technique in a Bach gigue.

EXAMPLE 9.6 Themes for Play & Continue practice.

only use themes that imply tonic harmony, thus avoiding for the moment the whole problem of getting two identical but asynchronous voices to agree on a chord progression. An easy way to transform Play & Hold themes into Play & Continue themes is merely to turn the long held note into several repeated notes. This is so simple it may seem like cheating!

EXERCISE: Return to the themes you invented to practice Play & Hold. Break all the held notes into repeated notes. There is no need to use a profusion of furious, quick rhythmic values. Just break the long note into two or three shorter notes. Notice that this simple Play & Continue technique creates a strong sense of continued activity in the first voice.

We may now proceed to add more pitches other than the held note broken up into repeated notes. Example 9.5 shows the opening of Bach's gigue from the F major English Suite. Here the composer employs the Play & Continue technique. The theme is made entirely of pitches from the tonic triad, and the continuation uses only ❶, but varies it by leaping up an octave. Despite the absolute simplicity of this harmonic plan, it nevertheless sounds active, complex, and interesting. The plainest of materials, managed well, can result in fine music.

EXERCISE: Using the themes from Example 9.6, create points of imitation employing the Play & Continue technique. You will need to invent the continuations for the themes. Limit your pitch choice to notes from the tonic triad. You need not use all three chord tones in every continuation; remember that a repeated single pitch can be just as effective. The continuation should be less active rhythmically than the answer in the second voice, since the continuation plays a supporting role at the moment of the answer's entry.

The next level of complexity is to imply changing harmonies within the theme and its answer. Even in composed music, harmonic progressions within imitation tend toward simplicity. Alternation between tonic and dominant is most common, and easiest to manage. We will begin with themes in which the first half implies tonic and the second half dominant. John Loeillet wrote just such a theme for the gigue from his E♭ suite. The two-measure theme consists of one bar of tonic followed by a bar of dominant. The answer enters with the same idea, while the first voice's continuation is made of simple chords. J. C. F. Fischer's C major gigue also alternates I and V, but each chord only lasts half a measure. Both points of imitation appear in Example 9.7.

EXERCISE: Example 9.8 provides five themes, each of which implies alternating I and V. Play the themes as written and add an answering voice in the left hand in a lower octave. Create a continuation for the upper voice that agrees with I and V and follows good voice-leading. Remember that thirds, sixths, and tenths are very safe. Contrary and oblique motion also work. Just avoid parallel

EXAMPLE 9.7   I and V in points of imitation.

EXAMPLE 9.8   Themes for imitation practice using I and V.

fifths and octaves. When you have created these solutions, place the themes in the left hand and imitate in the right hand. Transpose your points of imitation. Possible solutions are shown in Example 9.9.

EXERCISE: Write down your own themes that imply alternating I and V. If necessary, write out the continuation and answer's entrance. As soon as you are able, stop writing anything down and simply make up points of imitation at the piano. Practice starting every theme in either hand, and in several different keys.

No amount of writing on paper will fully prepare you to improvise fluently at the keyboard. You must keep practicing points of imitation until they seem easy. Do not be discouraged if you feel clumsy and slow for a while. Improvisation is a skill, not a gift, and you will certainly improve if you persist and do not give up.

Other harmonies are possible besides I and V. I and IV work, as well. Example 9.10 shows some themes constructed around tonic and subdominant.

EXERCISE: Create points of imitation on tonic and subdominant using the themes from Example 9.10. Try the themes starting in each hand and in several keys.

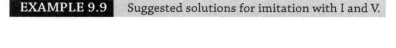

EXAMPLE 9.9   Suggested solutions for imitation with I and V.

EXAMPLE 9.10   Themes using I and IV.

We have studied a method of creating points of imitation using implied harmony. However, it is possible to manage points of imitation in two voices without thinking too specifically about an implied chord structure. In three or more voices, a chord progression of some kind is absolutely necessary, but two voices may proceed by using mostly imperfect consonances: thirds and sixths. It is true that two voices in imperfect consonances still imply harmony, but the improviser need not think about it too much. As long as the theme in one hand is accompanied primarily by thirds and sixths in the answer, the two-voice texture will sound correct.

This procedure of playing in two voices primarily in imperfect consonance is related to the sixteenth century pedagogical practice of *bicinium*. Bicinia were short exercises in two voices used for teaching counterpoint and singing. We will adopt the term for our technique of creating two-part keyboard music using mostly thirds and sixths. I recommend working on the following preliminary bicinium exercises before taking on further challenges.

> PRELIMINARY EXERCISE: Choose any key signature. Play up and down the piano with the right hand, staying within that key signature. Start with stepwise motion, and change direction frequently. Follow the right hand with the left a sixth below in parallel motion. Play in a wide variety of key signatures. Trade and let the left hand lead, with the right hand accompanying in sixths.
>
> PRELIMINARY EXERCISE: Do the same, but now using the interval of a tenth.
>
> PRELIMINARY EXERCISE: Do the same, but now the "following" hand will use sixths and tenths (and thirds, if convenient), changing frequently between these types of intervals. The point is not to create a masterpiece but to develop the skills of finding consonant intervals in real time. See Example 9.11

EXAMPLE 9.11 Solution for third preliminary exercise.

I made up the soprano first, then improvised the bass to go with it.

Here the soprano line is moved to the bass, and a new soprano is improvised.

2:1 Rules

We will now play themes in quarter notes and accompany them in eighth notes, for a ratio of 1:2. We must figure out what the second eighth—the "in between" note—should do. How do we fill in that space? The tradition of counterpoint pedagogy employs some rules that are useful for the improviser. In the case of 1:2 counterpoint, the rules are as follows:

- To fill between repeated notes, play a neighbor tone (usually lower).
- To fill between thirds, add a passing tone between them.
- For remaining intervals (including seconds), the filler note should jump a third toward the subsequent note.
- If any of these rules gets you into trouble, substitute some other consonant interval.

Example 9.12 illustrates these rules. As you can see, this is just another application of the principles of diminution, which we have already studied.

EXERCISE: Example 9.13 shows some themes. Play them while adding a second voice in the other hand. Maintain one note in the added voice for every note in the written voice (a 1:1 ratio between the hands). Choose notes for the second voice by using thirds and sixths away from the notes in the first voice. Octaves and fifths are acceptable, but not in parallel. Don't stay with the same interval for too long; while harmonious, it's not so interesting, and the goal of bicinium is to create independent lines. Example 9.14 provides sample solutions.

EXERCISE: Revisit the themes from Example 9.13. Accompany them with two notes in the second voice for every one note in the theme (2:1), using

EXAMPLE 9.12   Rules for 2:1 bicinium.

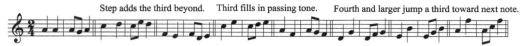

EXAMPLE 9.13   Themes for 1:1 bicinium practice.

EXAMPLE 9.14   Possible solutions for 1:1 bicinium exercise.

EXAMPLE 9.15   Possible solutions for 2:1 bicinium exercise.

the technique explained previously. Trade between the hands. Transpose. Example 9.15 shows some possible solutions.

EXERCISE: Practice creating points of imitation using bicinium technique. Choose a theme and play it in one hand. When it appears in the other hand as an answer, the first hand must accompany the answer by the rules of bicinium. Try this with many themes, and let the hands take turns as theme and answer. Transpose to many other keys.

Fake Stretto

Eighteenth-century musicians viewed *stretto* as a refined and sophisticated element of composition. Stretto occurs when a theme overlaps itself in very close

EXAMPLE 9.16   Stretto.

proximity; new entrances of the theme appear before the previous entrance has finished, and several staggered presentations of the theme may overlap. The term stretto is Italian for "narrow," as if the voices have encountered a narrow passageway and are forced to pile on top of each other.

True stretto, in which the theme appears in its fullness in all voices, is not a task for beginning improvisers due to the obligation to track three or four separate instances of the theme, all with different starting and ending points.

However, a technique I call *fake stretto* creates a similar effect and is much easier to handle. In fake stretto we present only the beginning of the theme in each voice. Because subsequent voices, entering with the same thematic fragment, divert the listener's attention from the previous voice, the listener doesn't notice that the theme was never completed in the previous voice.

In order to create a fake stretto we need a good chord progression. Let's use the Page One. We will then "tattoo" a thematic fragment onto various voices of the progression, creating the impression of stretto. Example 9.16 illustrates this procedure.

Notice that a thematic fragment that outlines a third is especially useful as it can fit within one chord. Fragments that are essentially decorated unisons are very easy to use as well. Sixths will work most of the time, although they take up more space and make the spacing of your chords more difficult. Fifths and fourths will give you lots of trouble, and sevenths are also a pain. Notice that it is not necessary to retain the exact intervals of the theme. In the eighth measure of Example 9.16 the alto line changes some intervals. It still sounds like the theme, because listeners do not identify tunes by exact interval but rather by rhythm and general shape.

EXERCISE: Example 9.17 shows four familiar chord progressions followed by a variety of themes. From each theme, take a fragment. You need not use the beginning of each theme; instead, choose a fragment that is rhythmically interesting, short, and will fit within a single chord. Then tattoo your fragment on various voices within each progression. Chord progressions may require metrical adjustment to accommodate the themes. The end of Example 9.17 shows one possible solution for the second progression matched with the first theme. Notice that the solution includes instances of changing the intervals of the theme fragment. When you can confidently create fake stretto with these themes and progressions, transpose them to more keys.

EXAMPLE 9.17   Themes and progressions for fake stretto.

EXERCISE: Choose one of your favorite chord progressions. Choose or create some short themes with catchy rhythmic qualities. Extract fragments from these themes and create fake stretto with your progression. Continue this exercise in a wide variety of keys and meters until you are confident with the skill of fake stretto.

Now that we can create points of imitation, we will connect them with longer pieces. We will look at how to do this specifically as the beginning of a gigue.

Gigues of the eighteenth century often begin with short points of imitation. Some go on as complete fugues, but many break off into free composition after the initial contrapuntal event. Example 9.18 shows the opening of Händel's gigue from the suite in D minor (HWV 449), which opens with a point of imitation in two voices before breaking off into free composition.

EXAMPLE 9.18   Händel's gigue from HWV 449.

EXAMPLE 9.19   Niedt progression with several levels of imitation.

EXAMPLE 9.20 Three types of themes useful for imitation.

We may attach a point of imitation to the beginning of a gigue in this manner. As we have already studied gigues using Niedt's method, all that remains is to meld the point of imitation with the main body of the gigue. As long as the point of imitation concludes on tonic harmony, we may move directly into the main body of the gigue without much trouble. Example 9.19 shows the first few bars of the Niedt progression, a possible realization in simple gigue texture, a theme, a point of imitation on that theme, and finally the point of imitation integrated with the rest of the gigue.

When starting gigues with points of imitation, I recommend three kinds of themes. The first outlines the tonic harmony only. While it may include brief passing or neighboring tones, on the whole it can be taken as a I chord. The second type implies alternating tonic and dominant, such as the theme from Example 9.19. Finally, the theme can be built on an ascending or descending scale. Scales easily "chase" each other if they are at an imperfect interval at the moment of the answer's entrance. Example 9.20 shows each of these types of themes, with answers.

EXERCISE: If necessary, go back to the chapter on suite and review the Niedt progression as applied to gigues. Prepare to improvise a complete gigue with the Niedt method. Select a theme similar to those shown in Example 9.20. Practice points of imitation on that theme integrated with a complete gigue. Make a note of complications you encounter when tying the imitation to the rest of the gigue, and work on solutions to those problems. Make it a habit to start all your improvised gigues with brief points of imitation.

When you find points of imitation that are interesting, copy them into your zibaldone. Make notes on how the themes function. Do they imply one chord only, or more? How complex are the continuations? How obvious are the underlying chord progressions?

Partimento

A partimento is a bass line, a puzzle, a potential composition, a homework assignment, and possibly one of the secret weapons behind the astonishing fluency of eighteenth-century musicianship. Scholars suggest that partimenti were foundational in the pedagogical systems of Baroque music, first in Italy and eventually across Europe.

We do not know all the details of the partimento training system because so much was passed on through oral tradition from master to apprentice. Students probably learned to decode partimenti at sight, like playing figured bass. But partimenti also served as prompts for more elaborate compositions, the way jazz musicians read from a chart. At times partimenti were also completed on paper. Intriguingly, they seem to have implied not just chords but polyphony, and even points of imitation, in the upper voices.

Ordinary figured bass serves as a shorthand intended for use in performance. Partimenti, on the other hand, are graded exercises posing deliberate harmonic and contrapuntal challenges. More advanced partimenti have few or even no figures at all; the musician had to figure it out independently. Part of the purpose was to train students to recognize patterns in the bass that imply complete voice-leading structures in the upper parts. A well-trained partimento player could glance at a few phrases of a bass line and quickly play several polyphonic possibilities in three or four voices.

This differs significantly from the approach to musicianship taught over the last one hundred years. The use of Roman numeral analysis and (for contemporary music) commercial chords symbols suggests to the student that each chord is a thing unto itself, a sonority that can be named and heard in isolation. The contemporary practice of referring to chords by the root, while useful within its own traditions, further reinforces the idea in modern minds that chords are chunks of sound rather than moments within a longer polyphonic process.

Let us suppose that at a certain point in a piece of music, the bass sounds E, and upper voices sound C, G and B. The modern student is likely to go figure that this is Cmaj7/E, and that such a description of a chunk of sound adequately explains this moment of music.

That is not how eighteenth-century musicians would have observed the same moment. Those trained in partimento would look immediately before and after the E in the bass to find out what kind of bass motion is going on. The meaning and function of the E would derive from its position within the bass motion—whether it was part of a scale, a series of leaps, or a cadential formula. The upper voices are a consequence of the bass motion.

Those looking for a comprehensive treatment of the partimento tradition should read Giorgio Sanguinetti's *The Art of Partimento: History, Theory, and Practice* (Oxford University Press, 2012).

Improvisers will profit from a study of partimento for several reasons. First, improvisation is founded upon bass motions. Partimenti are made of bass motions and thus have an obvious connection to the improviser's modes of thought.

Second, bass motions, like wild animals, can be tricky to observe in their natural habitat. Many bass motions are fleeting in real music—they begin but then abbreviate partway through and move on to some other motion. Partimenti provide a simplified pedagogical context in which students may encounter this "natural habitat" quality, like a wildlife preserve.

Third, partimenti present bass motions (and therefore harmonic realizations) as the masters actually played and taught them, not as reinterpreted by later generations.

Fourth, partimenti are graded in difficulty so that the beginner can start with only cadences and Rule of the Octave. In more advanced examples, the player gets less help from figures and must solve the partimento with knowledge of bass motions.

Finally, partimenti allow for expansive treatment and adventurous development, all within stylistic parameters.

For the improviser, partimenti hold intriguing promise. Any improviser would desire the ability to construct a full polyphonic texture, in real time at the keyboard, from a few hints in the bass. At the same time, we do not know precisely how the partimento training system worked, as no one has yet discovered an exhaustive written guide from the eighteenth century. We do have several treatises, each useful in its own way, but no single master covered every contingency nor explained in detail how to work with partimenti. Therefore, this chapter represents my own ideas about how improvisers might engage with the partimento tradition. We will study rules, bass motions, and partimento examples of Fedele Fenaroli and Giacomo Insanguine. After learning bass motions in abstract form, we will recognize those same motions in partimenti, realize the upper voices, and finally stylize the progressions with keyboard techniques. In my estimation, this process of "recognize, realize, stylize" can be a fruitful way to approach partimenti.

Some bass motions from Fenaroli and Insanguine will be familiar from previous chapters. The Circle of Fifths (C5), for example, we have already covered in detail. However, the partimento tradition represents a different way of thinking about and using these motions, so at the risk of revisiting familiar ground, we will take let these eighteenth-century masters guide us on their own terms.

The Three Cadences

While we have discussed cadences before, we have done so from a modern perspective, often describing them as ii-V-I. This is not how the partimento tradition views them, so we must revisit cadences with a bit more historic accuracy. In partimento, there is no such thing as perfect, imperfect, authentic, and inauthentic cadences, and Roman numerals are not used. A cadence only occurs when the bass moves from ⑤ to ①, and ① is on a stronger beat.

There are three types of cadences: simple, compound, and double. A simple cadence has two events: the bass, on ⑤, takes a chord of the fifth, then moves to ① and takes a chord of the fifth. Because this cadence has two events, it usually happens on two beats (often two quarter notes).

A compound cadence has three events. Over ⑤ in the bass, the upper voices first play a suspended chord (usually a fourth above the bass), then a resolved chord of the fifth, and finally the bass moves to ① and takes a chord of the fifth. Because of the greater number of events, compound cadences often take place over longer bass notes in partimenti.

The double cadence has five events. The first four events take place over ⑤ in the bass: a chord of the fifth, a six-four, a five-four (suspension), and a chord of the fifth. For the last event, ① in the bass takes a chord of the fifth. Double cadences very frequently take place over whole notes. If you see a whole note on ⑤ followed by ① on the following downbeat, chances are very good that it should be realized as a double cadence. The three types of cadences according to Fenaroli are illustrated in Example 10.1.

EXAMPLE 10.1   Fenaroli's cadences.

EXERCISE: Learn the cadences according to Fenaroli's model, and then figure them out in all three starting positions of the soprano. Transpose to many other keys, including minor.

Partimenti initiate modulations through *scale mutations*, which are simply chromatic alterations. Very often the altered note is the leading tone of the new key (if moving in the sharps direction) or the cancelation of the same (if moving toward flats). The scale mutation may appear in the bass, as a figure, or may not appear at all but be implied by the motion of the bass. Of course, notes aside from leading tones may change, as well. In more advanced partimenti, the player will be left to figure out where the scale mutation should take place.

The Moves of the Partimento

Most eighteenth-century masters taught cadences and Rule of the Octave first. Since we have already studied both these techniques, we are ready to look at Fenaroli's first partimento. (If you need to review either topic, please refer to the appropriate chapters.)

We will realize partimenti on six levels.

1. Recognize all bass motions, scale mutations, and cadences, labeling them if necessary.
2. Play the partimento as chords.
3. Turn the chords into a figuration pattern, using chord tones only.
4. Play as chords with diminutions in one or more voices.
5. Melt the upper voices into a flowing line in a compound melody style, where a single line touches on all the important pitches and implies a full harmony.
6. Transform the partimento into another kind of piece by devices such as changing the meter, using dance rhythms, and adding keyboard figuration in various styles.

Example 10.2 shows the first partimento exercise by Fenaroli. It looks no different from a standard figured bass line we might encounter in continuo

EXAMPLE 10.2 Fenaroli's first partimento.

playing. However, a partimento has specific pedagogical purposes. Fenaroli wants us to figure out which bass notes represent cadential formulae, and which ones should be harmonized by Rule of the Octave. In order to solve the first partimento, we need cadences, RO, and the ability to recognize key changes by means of scale mutations.

EXERCISE: Copy Fenaroli's first partimento into your zibaldone. Label sections of the partimento where you find cadences, key changes, and RO. Play it at the piano in a simple chordal texture using two or three voices in the right hand. Do not let the soprano form parallel fifths or octaves with the bass, and make sure every chord includes the intervals Fenaroli specifies. Don't write down this chordal version; just play. Take note of the key changes. Transpose the partimento. These activities represent the first two levels of realization.

Don't be confused by the third beat of the first measure, where the C takes a chord of the fifth (but according to RO should be a ⁶₅). In this case, because ④ does not continue up to ⑤, it can take a chord of the fifth. Fenaroli, Furno, and others taught that ④ had the option of taking the chord of the fifth *when not proceeding to nor from* ⑤. ⑥ has the option of the chord of the fifth *when not descending to* ⑤ nor ascending to ⑦. However, ④ and ⑥ can take the usual ⁶₅ in these circumstances, as well. Either will work. I call this the ④-⑥ *exception*. Note that ⑤ to ⑥ in the bass (what we call a deceptive cadence) could both take chords of the fifth, if parallels are avoided and ⑥ does not proceed to ⑦.

Example 10.3 shows the identification of bass motions, cadences, and modulations. Example 10.4 shows a solution for chords in four voices.

EXERCISE: Play the partimento using figuration. In order to create a consistent figuration pattern, you will need to decide whether to use two or three upper voices. When you can play at a steady tempo with figuration, transpose to other keys.

EXAMPLE 10.3   Fenaroli's first partimento with motions, modulations, and cadences identified.

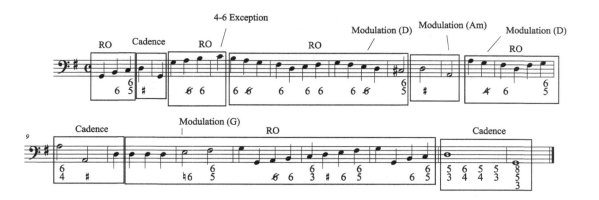

EXAMPLE 10.4   Realization in four voices of Fenaroli's first partimento.

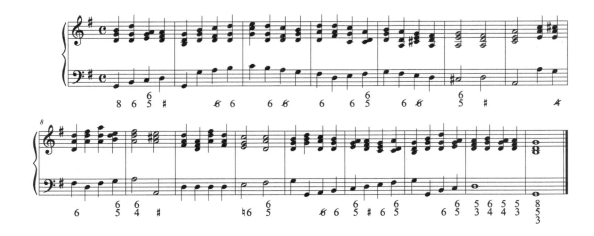

EXAMPLE 10.5   Nonharmonic tones added to Fenaroli's first partimento.

We have now done the first three levels of realization. At the fourth level we return to a chordal texture, but add diminutions where possible. The easiest place to do so is wherever you find intervals of a third. Simply add a stepwise note on the offbeat, filling in the interval. You may also add a neighbor tone to any note that repeats. Most voices that move by step may be suspended.

EXERCISE: Add diminutions to your partimento realization. For now, add them to the upper voices only, leaving the bass as written. Play it several times, changing your diminutions every time. Example 10.5 provides a possible solution for the first four measures.

EXERCISE: Using the same partimento, develop a right-hand part consisting of a single voice moving in constant eighth notes. Because you have two right-hand notes for every note in the bass, you can include two upper voices in your line. You need not always put the soprano on the beat and the alto on the offbeat; switch them up and try to create an interesting, meandering line that creates harmonic fullness while presenting an interesting melodic contour. Transpose the partimento to other keys. When you are confident with eighth notes, try sixteenths. With sixteenth-notes you can touch on a hypothetical "third voice" or simply create more nonharmonic tones. EXAMPLE 10.6 provides some ideas for the first four measures.

EXAMPLE 10.6   Fenaroli's first partimento realized with a single upper voice.

EXAMPLE 10.7   Fenaroli's first partimento as a sarabande.

EXAMPLE 10.8   Fenaroli's second partimento.

The sixth level of partimento realization resembles Niedt's method for playing suite movements from a given bass. At this level, you are completely free to expand and contract durations, change meters, and add any kind of surface figuration.

EXERCISE: Review the procedures for improvising suite movements from Chapter 8. While Fenaroli's partimento is not in the form of a suite movement, you can style play it in the style of an allemande, sarabande, or any dance. Try the rhythms and textures of various suite movements. You may also play it as an unmeasured prelude, a figuration prelude, a free toccata, a slow lyrical piece, or any other way you imagine. As you try out these different styles, transpose to other keys. Example 10.7 shows an idea for transforming this partimento into a sarabande.

A remarkable array of pieces may evolve from just one partimento—and with only cadences, modulations, and RO. Fenaroli's second partimento, shown in Example 10.8, also limits itself these same techniques. Near the end we see an instance in which the bass moves by faster rhythmic values. The player must discern if these each require harmonization, or some are diminutions and may be ignored. The antepenultimate measure contains four running eighths, which may be harmonized merely as though the bass were ①. Or we could harmonize all of them, very quickly, as RO.

EXERCISE: Apply the six levels of realization to Fenaroli's second partimento. Copy it into your zibaldone and mark the cadences, bass motions, and modulations. Play as simple chords. Play as figuration using only chord tones. Play as chords with diminutions. Play the upper voices as a compound melodic line. Finally, transform it into other kinds of pieces. Transpose at every level of realization. The first four measures of Example 10.9 show the partimento as a figuration prelude, measures 5–8 with compound melody, and the remaining bars transformed into a rather ambitious allemande.

EXAMPLE 10.9   Fenaroli's second partimento with figuration, compound melody, and as an allemande.

EXAMPLE 10.10 Insanguine's second partimento.

Insanguine's second partimento, seen in Example 10.10, consists of nearly constant eighth notes. The players first task is to recognize which are structural and which are decorative. Octave leaps are almost always decorative; indeed, the four-note pattern with the octave leap followed by a third (e.g., the first measure) may stand for a single note. Insanguine's figures affirm this impression. The third measure, in the which the bass arpeggiates D minor tonality, may be treated as a single bass note (D) and harmonized accordingly.

The first two measures bounce between tonic and dominant harmonies before reaching a cadence at the end of measure 2 and beginning of 3. When the harmony alternates between tonic and dominant but does not convey a sense of closure, I like to refer to it as a Tonic-Dominant Oscillation (TDO). The purpose of using a different term is to distinguish it from a cadence, which does not normally repeat itself.

I am not aware of any eighteenth-century master who taught the TDO as a distinct bass motion. Because it is as natural and frequent in music as breathing, they may have taken it for granted. In their world, little could be more obvious and self-explanatory than rocking back and forth between these two tonalities. Nevertheless, it serves our purposes as improvisers to notice, name, and study this phenomenon as we would any other bass motion.

The voice-leading of the upper parts has many options; as long as you avoid parallels and don't double the leading tone, you are free to use any upper lines as you see fit. However, some partimenti have figures in a very specific order, not the highest-to-lowest order we expect. This means that the master may intend that the upper voices should be arranged precisely as the figures indicate. The reason for this level of detail is to show the player some fine point of voice-leading. When the figures are unusually particular, follow their suggestions to discover whether a specific voice leading idea will appear. A word of caution: in some cases, figures may appear to be purposefully "upside down" but result in wrong voice leading. In such cases, just find good solutions without regard to the order of the figures.

This partimento requires another bass motion: the C5, which we know already. When Insanguine introduces the C5 bass motion in his treatise he immediately recommends the use of sevenths in the harmonization. Here in the second partimento, he writes several circles. The first one uses triadic harmony only, while others employ sevenths. The dissonant sevenths must be prepared by common tone and resolved by step. The upper voice-leading for this motion is easy and convenient, as shown in Example 10.11. The third and seventh of any chord reverse roles and become the seventh and third of the next chord.

Measure 6 of the partimento begins with a cadence in F major and immediate begins a stepwise descent. We might expect that the F tonality would continue, and this stepwise motion would be harmonized by RO. However, the ♯6 on beat 3 says otherwise. Further, the scale descends to C♯ on the downbeat of measure 7. These two bits of evidence indicate that we are in D minor. Therefore, this descending scale should receive RO harmonization in that key, not in F. A surprise jump to G♯ means that once again we are changing key. The partimento player has to stay alert for such unexpected obstacles.

The pattern in measure 20 implies two voices: a lower pedal point on ⑤, and a higher voice sounding ❶ and ❼. This is best understood as a TDO over a dominant pedal. The upper parts could include a voice moving in parallel motion with ❶ and ❼ helping to fill out the TDO harmony.

Measure 21 descends through a complete scale and has no figures. Harmonization will depend partly on tempo. At quicker speed, it is possible to consider this entire measure as D minor, with the scale serving as decoration. Perhaps this is Insanguine's intention, given the lack of figures. Still, at a more moderate tempo, a long tonic chord could sound plodding. A complete RO is possible, as is harmonization by fauxbourdon (parallel first-inversion chords). If you need to review fauxbourdon, please see the chapter on toccata.

Measure 22 presents a common strategy known as Indugio (see the chapter on schemata for more on this). The Indugio prolongs the predominant harmony

EXAMPLE 10.11   Voice-leading for a C5 progression with sevenths.

and stirs it up with rhythmic activity. For this Indugio the upper voices could include parallel or contrary motion with the bass. For the overall harmony of the measure, consider the bass to be ④, which takes ⁶₅.

A few "correct" figures are missing from this partimento. The player will need to recognize when an accidental is required, or an extra note should be added to a chord.

EXERCISE: Copy Insanguine's second partimento into your zibaldone. Label the bass motions, cadences, and modulations. Realize with chords, with figuration using only chord tones, and play as chords with passing tones. Create a compound melodic line for the upper voices. Change anything you want and play in other styles. Transpose at every level of realization. Example 10.12 provides a few measures of realization in a simple chordal texture.

Insanguine's third partimento, shown in Example 10.13, introduces a few new motions. In the second measure, the bass descends a third from C to A, then rises a step to B. This motion, which descends a third and rises a second, is very common. It normally appears with more repetitions of the pattern. We will address it more fully when it shows up again in Insanguine's eleventh partimento. For now, harmonize according to the figures given. If you follow his figures exactly, matching the soprano note according to the top of each set of figures, dissonances will not be correctly prepared and resolved, so we have to conclude that the order in which the figures are "stacked" is not meant to be literal.

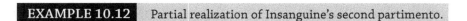

EXAMPLE 10.12   Partial realization of Insanguine's second partimento.

EXAMPLE 10.13   Insanguine's third partimento.

EXAMPLE 10.14   Voice-leading for a tied bass sequence.

The other new motion appears in measures 7 and 8 over the tied descending bass line. This is where we deploy the $^6_3$-$^4_2$ (also known as tied bass). As the name implies, the pattern alternates between chords of the sixth and second. One voice-leading solution is shown in Example 10.14.

A tied bass (or a long note spanning the middle of a measure) usually implies a bass suspension. That's what a $^4_2$ chord is. The bass note itself is the dissonance, and must fall to resolve, resulting in a descending scale. According to Insanguine's figures, we should go directly from the B chord into the $^4_2$ on the downbeat of measure 8. After the cadence in measure 9, you should be able to identify and solve the C5 progression that follows. In measures 6–7, Insanguine does not provide figures for what is obviously a cadence. Partimento teachers gradually left out figures so that players could work them out independently.

Insanguine's original third partimento sometimes used four figures and sometimes three. For the sake of simplicity I have changed the partimento to no more than three figures (and therefore three upper voices) throughout.

EXERCISE: Apply the six levels of realization to Insanguine's third partimento. Example 10.15 shows several approaches to realization, from simple chords to complex imitative textures.

Insanguine's sixth partimento offers a chance to try out several familiar bass motions: the C5, Ascending 5-6, and the Descending 7-6. Since we have studied all these motions previously, we will not review them here. Further, Insanguine leaves out several figures and writes in sixteenth notes, requiring the player to exercise significant judgment about what the harmonizations are, and where they occur. Example 10.16 shows the partimento.

Note that if we take the figures in measures 19–20 literally, we would place the seventh in the top voice all the time, in contrast to stepwise voice-leading, where thirds and sevenths trade places. I think it unlikely that Insanguine intended this; the order of figures from top to bottom is not always reliable. Harmonize this section using the normal voice-leading of thirds and sevenths.

EXERCISE: Apply the six levels of realization to the sixth partimento of Insanguine.

EXAMPLE 10.15   Various ideas for realizing Insanguine's third partimento.

EXAMPLE 10.16   Insanguine's sixth partimento.

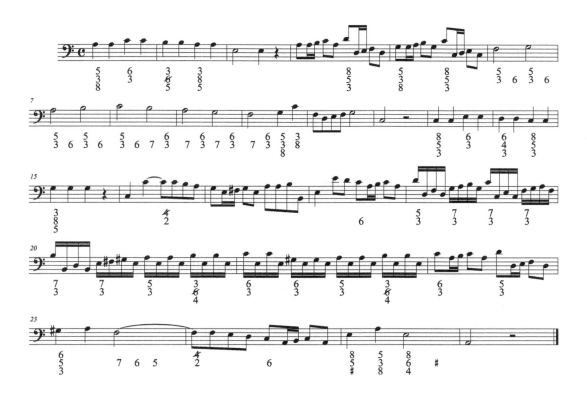

EXAMPLE 10.17   Fenaroli's fourth partimento.

EXAMPLE 10.18   Fenaroli's solutions for a descending chromatic bass line.

Fenaroli's fourth partimento, shown in Example 10.17, introduces two chromatic motions: one falling and one rising.

For unknown reasons, the rising bass motion receives the same harmonization Fenaroli taught in his treatise, but the falling pattern does not. In this partimento, the falling bass receives a simplified harmonization of a sixth and third, not unlike a fauxbourdon with chromatic passing tones in the bass. Perhaps this was a compromise for students, who would be expected to learn to complete version later. A bass descending chromatically from ① to ⑤ in minor is often called *Lamento*, and frequently appears in music associated with sorrow, such as the Crucifixus from J. S. Bach's Mass in B minor.

The descending motion works the same way every time it appears in this partimento: The bass always moves from ① down to ⑤, and the upper voices take a third and sixth above the bass. Or, if you wish to solve this motion with either of the harmonizations from Fenaroli's treatise (which is also the same as Bach's Crucifixus), see Example 10.18.

EXAMPLE 10.19   Ideas for realizing Fenaroli's fourth partimento.

The ascending motion is sometimes known as the Monte. You can read about it in detail in the chapter on schemata. The chromatic notes take $^6_5$ chords, while the diatonic notes take $^5_3$ chords.

EXERCISE: Apply the six levels of realization to Fenaroli's fourth partimento. Example 10.19 provides some ideas for solutions.

Insanguine's eighth partimento, shown in Example 10.20, presents more new challenges. In measures 17–19 he asks for the down-third-up-second motion. The pattern normally starts on a $^5_3$ chord. As the bass drops a third it takes a $^6_3$ or $^6_5$. Fenaroli's treatise provides solutions, including one with some lovely suspensions. These are shown in Example 10.21.

In measure 8 we see the marking "imit.," indicating that the player is to initiate a point of imitation at that moment. We don't have all the facts about this practice. We may assume that some little thematic fragment (most likely the

EXAMPLE 10.20 Insanguine's eighth partimento.

EXAMPLE 10.21 Fenaroli's solutions for descending alternating thirds.

EXAMPLE 10.22 Ideas for realizing Insanguine's eighth partimento.

EXAMPLE 10.23 Insanguine's fifteenth partimento.

motive immediately before the "imit." marking) is the material for imitation. If that is the case, the player will repeat the four eighths from the end of measure 7 in an upper voice. I am further assuming that the indicated interval of a sixth (marked next to "imit.") is the interval at which fragment should appear above the bass.

EXERCISE: Apply the six levels of realization to Insanguine's eighth partimento. Example 10.22 provides possible solutions and includes ideas for the imitation.

Insanguine's fifteenth partimento, seen in Example 10.23, consists of sixteenth notes with no figures. At this point the master expected the student to figure out the whole piece. In that spirit, I invite you to do the same.

EXERCISE: Apply the six levels of realization to Insanguine's fifteenth partimento.

In your zibaldone, develop a collection of partimenti. Copy in the original versions and then write your own realizations, using techniques from each of the six levels. Practice realizing partimenti at sight, and as the mindset of partimento becomes clearer to you, write your insights in your zibaldone.

Schemata

Schemata are short patterns in two voices, normally melody and bass. They are closely related to bass motions. In the world of bass motions, the lowest voice is the foundation and upper voices are added to it. In schemata, however, the melody and bass are more or less equal in importance. Another difference is that eighteenth-century musicians taught bass motions formally and consistently, whereas schemata seem to be an unspoken but pervasive set of musical assumptions everybody held.

Each schema is flexible and may be subject to limitless decoration, expansion, and modification. They serve specific roles such as presentations, continuations, diversions, acceleration toward cadences, time-wasters, tension-builders, and any other narrative function that a good story might need. These are patterns we have heard and played our whole lives, although we may not have known them by name or stopped to consider them in detail.

We explain schemata as a series of events or stages. With each motion of the melody or bass note (or both), we reach a new stage of the schema. The stages may be very short, such as a single staccato note, or very long, such as a downbeat with a full measure of decorative notes before the next stage.

The significance of schemata is that they represent discrete musical thoughts or gestures. Music theory students today are trained in Roman analysis, which is useful but does not represent an actual mode of eighteen musical thought. Mozart did not create music by thinking, "I'll do a I chord. Now what? How about a V? Next let's do a vi." In the same way, Shakespeare did not write plays by thinking, "I shall write an L. And now perhaps the letter E, followed by A. What next, forsooth? R!"

Just as a playwright thinks not in individual letters but in phrases, so eighteenth-century composers thought not in single notes nor chords but in longer voice-leading patterns. This means that schemata have the potential to serve as powerful tools for improvisation, since they are precisely the gestures that musicians of the past in fact used. Individual chords go flashing by too quickly, and complete sections of pieces are too long to imagine in detail. Schemata, however, are just the right length to think of, and then play, in real time. They are useful in any meter, compressed or lengthened, in any key, with any imaginable surface figuration.

Schemata do not normally appear unadorned in real music. The notes of a schema are structural, meaning that they are the primary voice-leading pitches that determine what is happening harmonically. They may be buried under many other decorative notes. With practice, however, it is possible to hear schemata and identify them in scores. In this chapter we will learn to improvise using a limited selection of schemata within the clear framework of short pieces such as minuets.

Schemata appear in many styles of music. However, the specific schemata in this chapter are especially suitable for the galant style, that oft-overlooked era after Bach and before Beethoven. The sound of schemata improvisation, then, will be what many would call "early classical."

Much of the foundational scholarship on schemata comes from the work of Robert Gjerdingen. Interested readers should consult his *Music in the Galant Style* (Oxford University Press, 2007).

Before studying schemata in detail, you should build a personal library of stylistic keyboard techniques. Schemata give only sparse voice-leading information; the improviser must provide the keyboard textures that make the music sound convincing. For example, the bass line of a schema could be realized in staccato notes, octaves, broken octaves, Alberti patterns incorporating other voices, and in countless other ways. The schema itself does not provide this information; that is the responsibility of the improviser. I recommend writing down a collection of accompaniments, passagework, and ornamentation appropriate to the galant style. Your zibaldone is perfect for this task. To get you started, Example 11.1 provides a few common accompaniment patterns.

Benedetto Marcello's minuet is seen in Example 11.2 together with a version reduced only to the essential notes. In this reduced version, we can most easily find the schemata. The first four measures are made of a *Do-Re-Mi*. The Do-Re-Mi is an opener. It consists of ❶-❷-❸ in an upper voice, supported by ①-⑦-①, ①-⑤-①, ①-⑤-⑦-① (as seen here), or something similar, in the bass. Thus, it is a three-stage schema. Example 11.1 really has a Do-Re-Re-Mi, a frequent variant, which is a four-stage schema. (Schemata are flexible like that.) The Do-Re-Re-Mi variant is perfect fit: four events to fit within four measures. Note that

EXAMPLE 11.1 Common accompaniment patterns.

EXAMPLE 11.2   Benedetto Marcello's minuet.

due to the scale degree combinations, the Do-Re-Mi will almost certainly have a I-V-I harmony, which is appropriate for an opening phrase.

As the Marcello begins, the bass line consists only of the same pitch repeated for a full measure, so we have no elaborative notes to ignore. In the melody, however, the schema notes occur once per measure, and are surrounded by elaboration. In most of the Marcello the downbeat note is schematic, except for measures 2 and 4, in which suspensions and neighboring tones prevent the schematic note from coming to rest until beat 3.

As we work with schemata, we must develop the skill of seeing beyond the elaborative notes to the underlying structural pitches. Once you have taken away everything decorative, what you have left is schemata. Schemata are cement blocks and two-by-fours. Elaborative notes are carpets and pictures and chairs.

EXERCISE: Play measures 1–4 of the Marcello and the same section of the template. Do this several times until you can hear the Do-Re-Re-Mi schema underneath Marcello's original phrase.

The *Prinner* is a schema that answers an opener and therefore serves as a continuation or *riposte*. It normally consists of ❻-❺-❹-❸ in an upper voice, supported by ④-③-②-① in the bass: two voices moving in parallel tenths. You can also think of it as a IV chord that walks back down to a I chord. Measures 5–8 of Example 11.1 display a Prinner, but it only makes sense if you think of it in the key of G (where the C in the bass would be ④). This is known as a *Modulating Prinner*, a very common device. (We will study the "normal" Prinner in due course.) Marcello uses the Modulating Prinner to approach the half cadence at the end of the A section. A defining characteristic of the Prinner is its stepwise descending parallel voices in 10ths.

EXERCISE: Play measures 5–8 of the Marcello and the corresponding section of the template until you can hear that the downbeats of each measure consist of the schematic notes.

The *Fonte* is a bit more adventurous harmonically. The upper voice is often ❺-❹-❹-❸, although in Example 11.1 it's ❸-❹-❷-❸. The bass, though, is the key to the Fonte: ♯①-②-⑦-①. The leading tone of ii leads to ii. Then the leading tone of I leads to I. So it seems to undertake a short but daring modulation to ii but immediate regrets the indiscretion and returns to I. Fontes are common at the beginning of B sections of minuets and other short bipartite pieces, as we see in Marcello's piece.

EXERCISE: Play the Fonte sections of the Marcello and template, observing how the schema defines the passage.

The last four measures consist of the schema called *Grand*. The Grand is a cadence approached by ③ and ④ in the bass, often with a soprano descending from ❺.

EXERCISE: Play the last four measures of the original and template, listening for the schema that underlies the original.

From this exercise we discover that Marcello's minuet does not just contain schemata; it is *made* of them. Therefore, if we gain the ability to select and deploy schemata judiciously, elaborating them with stylistic surface decoration, it becomes possible to improvise complete pieces. First, however, we need to go back and study the schemata in greater detail, practice them in a simple texture, and learn how to elaborate them so they sound stylistically convincing.

Do-Re-Mi

We will look first at the Do-Re-Mi, so named because the melody follows the first three steps of the scale, while we hear ①-⑦-①, ①-⑤-①, or something similar in the bass. The Do-Re-Mi is most often encountered as an opening gesture, an announcement of a main theme at the beginning of a piece. See Example 11.3 for illustration of the Do-Re-Mi in abstract form and then as used in Haydn's Divertimento in C, Hob. XVI/7.

EXERCISE: Play the Do-Re-Mi in every major and minor key. Use ①-⑦-① or ①-⑤-① (or a combination of both) in the bass.

The Do-Re-Mi is easy to understand and play in its abstract form. However, schemata normally function as underlying structure, over which we hear decorative material, elaborative figuration, and keyboard gymnastics. This surface detail may be quite minimal, such as a little ornament on one note, or it could be dozens of notes hiding the schema beneath.

A Do-Re-Mi with minimal decoration may still be easy to detect. Haydn's D major sonata, Hob. XVI/51, is such an instance. The only "extra" notes are quick arpeggios of the chord tones of I and V. Example 11.4 shows this theme as well as Kozeluch's sonata in B♭, Op. 2, a similarly transparent use of the Do-Re-Mi.

Example 11.5 shows two selections from sonatas of Cimarosa. In both cases, the downbeats of the right hand consist of structural notes. The remainder of each measure confirms the tonic and dominant chords. While hearing the Do-Re-Mi in these examples is not too difficult, one needs to sense the greater importance of the downbeats in order to perceive the schema. Note also that the second example lengthens the schema by doubling the first two stages: Do-Do-Re-Re-Mi, as it were. The third selection in the example is from the second sonata of the Marquise de Montalembert. Once again the listener must pick up on the downbeats to perceive the schema. The final selection is from the third

EXAMPLE 11.3   The Do-Re-Mi.

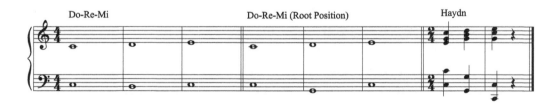

EXAMPLE 11.4   Do-Re-Mi in Haydn's Hob. XVI/51 and Kozeluch's Op. 2.

EXAMPLE 11.5   Do-Re-Mi in Cimarosa, Montalembert, and Vento.

sonata of Mathias Vento. In Vento's piece we must disregard downbeats because they are nonharmonic tones delaying the arrival of the actual structural note. The schema notes are marked (*). Vento here inserts an extra stage with the soprano on the leading tone; we could call this Do-Re-(Ti)-Mi. The bass, meanwhile, is very simple: ①-⑤-⑤-①.

EXERCISE: Play the Do-Re-Mi in a wide variety of keys. Employ surface embellishments to make the schema sound like real music. Draw upon your knowledge of keyboard literature, and steal elaboration ideas from your favorite composers. Try variants of the schema such as Do-Re-Re-Mi. Use ⑤ or ⑦ (or both) in the bass. "Hide" the schema by using nonharmonic tones in the melody. Example 11.6 provides some ideas for embellishment. In the example, schema notes in the soprano are marked (*).

After starting with an opener such as the Do-Re-Mi, we may respond with an answering phrase such as the Prinner. The Prinner is defined by parallel tenths (or thirds) between soprano and bass, walking down by step. The bass moves from ④ to ① while the soprano moves from ❻ to ❸. In many cases the Prinner implies a IV chord walking down to a I chord. Example 11.7 shows the Prinner in simple, abstract form followed by the opening of a movement from Giovanni Platti's Sonata No. 1. Platti begins with a Do-Re-Mi followed by a Prinner. The Do-Re-Mi is well hidden: many filler notes separate each structural note, and the structural notes in the soprano are delayed by suspensions. His Prinner, on the other hand, is more obvious, with the schema notes falling on every downbeat.

EXAMPLE 11.6 Ideas for embellishing the Do-Re-Mi.

EXAMPLE 11.7 Examples of Prinners.

EXERCISE: Play simple, abstract Prinners in every major and minor key. Then try elaborating your own Prinners with stylistically appropriate devices such as ornaments, diminutions, arpeggios, and scales. Finally, practice combining your own Do-Re-Mis and Prinners into longer phrases. Transpose to many keys. Example 11.8 shows a Do-Re-Mi/Prinner combination I made up. The schema notes are not marked; try to identify them yourself.

The Prinner usually begins with the bass on ④ and the soprano on ❻. However, it may begin in another place, with different harmonic results. If the soprano walks down from ❸ to ❼ while the bass moves from ① down to ⑤, the implication is that a I chord has walked down to a V chord. This is the Modulating Prinner we first saw in the Marcello (Example 11.2). The Modulating Prinner may follow an opener such as the Do-Re-Mi. Because the Prinner is a four-stage schema, it does not fit evenly in meters such as $\frac{3}{4}$. In $\frac{3}{4}$ you must shorten the second and fourth stages if you wish to fit within two measures. If the Prinner is to last four measures, you may take a full measure for each stage of the schema.

EXERCISE: Improvise simple Do-Re-Mi and Modulating Prinner combinations. Elaborate them with stylistic decoration. Transpose to other keys.

In this style of music, phrases culminate in cadences. The improviser needs several types of cadence ready for quick deployment. The half-cadence comes to rest on V. It may or may not tonicize V by using the leading tone of V (♯④ in the home key), but either way the cadence should sound temporary, not conclusive. You may go directly to V from I, but half cadences often approach from ④ in the bass. The half-cadence in Example 11.8 works this way: the bass rises from ① to ⑤ while the soprano agrees in parallel tenths. The half-cadence often appears at the end of the A section of short bipartite pieces. It allows for a brief pause in the action, and sets the harmony up either to return to the tonic (if taking the repeat) or move forward to new territory (in the B section).

EXERCISE: Improvise Do-Re-Mi/Prinner combinations concluding with half-cadences. Play in many keys and various meters.

In addition to half-cadences, the improviser needs full cadences, as well, with motion of V-I in root position. A perfect authentic cadence will place the soprano on ❶ on the final chord. For our purposes in this chapter, it is not necessary to conclude everything with a first-position I chord, but pieces should end with V-I, both in root position. (Note that when working with schemata,

EXAMPLE 11.8   Do-Re-Mi/Prinner combination.

we need to use modern terminology to discuss things like root position, authentic cadences, and Roman numerals. This is one area where schemata and partimento are very different, and is the reason I treat them in separate chapters.)

EXERCISE: Review authentic cadences in every key. Start with V-I. Keep working until every cadence in every key is familiar. Learn the cadences in various positions of the right hand. Then add ii$^6_5$ chords before each cadence. You should be able to improvise authentic cadences in any key, any meter, and any position. (In my experience, the student improvisers who lack fluency are always the ones who don't work thoroughly on tasks like this.) I have decided not to provide any musical examples to help because figuring these cadences out for yourself is good for you.

A *Fonte* is a four-stage schema, with the first and third stages landing on strong beats. If each stage fills a complete measure, strong and weak placement is less important. The bass goes ♯①-②-⑦-①. The soprano usually follows ❺-❹-❹-❸ but may vary. The function of the Fonte is to depart from the home key very briefly before returning, like a quick day trip. The Fonte often appears at the beginning of the B section of a short work such as a minuet. Example 11.9 shows a Fonte in abstract form followed by two selections, each with a Fonte, from Fenaroli's Cembalo sonatas. In the Fenaroli, schematic notes are marked (*). Another way to think of this schema is as two dominant-tonic progressions: the first pair tonicizes ii; the second tonicizes I. The Roman analysis would be V$^6_5$/ii-ii-V$^6_5$-I. In contemporary chords the progression would be A7/C♯-Dm-G7/B-C (if in C major, of course).

EXERCISE: Play the abstract, two-voice Fonte from Example 11.9 and transpose it to several other keys. Then construct Fontes with the full harmony as described in the previous paragraph, first as block chords and then with stylistically appropriate figuration such as Alberti patterns, ornaments, and so on. Transpose to several other keys.

EXAMPLE 11.9   Examples of Fontes.

The *indugio* is a schema that delays a cadence by extending a pre-dominant harmony and imbuing it with rhythmic activity, thereby generating excitement and expectation. Most typically the chord is ii$_5^6$. The indugio may be of various lengths, but should convey a sense of delay in the harmonic progression. As it nears the dominant, the bass often rises chromatically ④-#④-⑤. Example 11.10 shows an indugio leading to a half-cadence from Mozart's familiar Sonata in C, K. 545, followed by examples of indugio ideas that could be useful for the improviser.

The indugio has no specific voice-leading for the soprano. Since rhythmic energy is required, the soprano probably has to run all over the place, anyway. A simple approach is to arpeggiate the ii$_5^6$ chord or to play scales that outline this harmony. Note that Mozart's indugio uses scales which always start and end on notes of the ii$_5^6$ chord.

EXERCISE: Improvise indugios that lead into cadences (both half and authentic). Try major and minor keys and various meters.

We now have enough schemata to improvise a short piece in bipartite form. Example 11.11 will serve as our template for these improvisations. The template has no time or key signature, since we will frequently change these.

EXAMPLE 11.10   Examples of Indugios.

EXAMPLE 11.11 Improvisation template.

However, we will follow the order of schemata as well the number of measures allotted to each. In this template, we allot only two measures for the Prinner, so you will not be able to use long, sprawling Prinners like Platti in Example 11.7, where the composer uses a full measure for each stage. Instead, you will need to fit two Prinner stages into each measure. The Do-Re-Re-Mi, on the other hand, will allow for a full measure for every stage of the schema, as will the Fonte.

You may wish to copy the template into your zibaldone and compose some pieces before improvising. Composition helps you understand the limitations of working within a specified number of measures, and will temporarily alleviate the pressure of creating music in real time.

EXERCISE: Improvise complete pieces using the template from Example 11.11. Allow yourself to pause between schemata if you need to think. Before attempting fully realized keyboard figuration, try them in two voices using only long note values. Gradually fill out the texture with stylistic elements as you gain confidence. Example 11.12 demonstrates a two-voice solution followed by a full (yet fairly simple) stylistic realization.

Scholars have identified several opening schemata in addition to the Do-Re-Mi. In this chapter we will learn the *Meyer, Jupiter, Aprile,* and *Romanesca.* The first three, like the Do-Re-Mi, outline tonic-dominant-tonic progressions and are shown in Example 11.13.

These opening schemata closely resemble each other, using a basic I-V-I strategy. All are very easy to decorate with stylistic embellishments, and sound like real music of the galant era.

EXERCISE: Improvise short phrases using the Meyer, Jupiter, and Aprile. When you are confident, improvise complete pieces using the plan from Example 11.12, substituting these new schemata in place of the Do-Re-Mi.

The Romanesca is an opener but does not follow a simple I-V-I plan. While the soprano line may take various shapes, the bass will descend as follows: ①-⑦-⑥-③. Some scholars suggest that the soprano may emphasize ❶ and ❺, but

EXAMPLE 11.12   Two-voice and compound melody solutions for the template.

EXAMPLE 11.13   The Meyer, Jupiter, and Aprile.

other melodic notes are certainly possible. Over the four bass notes, the harmony will alternate chords of the fifth and chords of the sixth. Example 11.14 shows a Romanesca.

The Romanesca concludes with the bass on ③. This is a good set-up for the Prinner, as the bass can move up a step to ④. Romanesca/Prinner combinations are common.

EXERCISE: Improvise Romanesca/Prinner combinations in a variety of keys. Example 11.15 provides an abstract outline of the combination followed by a possible solution.

EXERCISE: Improvise complete pieces on the template from Example 11.11, using a Romanesca in place of the Do-Re-Mi. Try various keys and meters. If you wish, change the allotment of measures to each schema. For example, you could play a more condensed Romanesca in two measures, then a longer Prinner of four measures.

The *Ponte* ("bridge") is a schema that tarries on the dominant. It may employ all inversions and positions of V, so an exact outline of the voice-leading cannot be specified. Still, the Ponte is easy to recognize due to its conspicuous loitering on and around the V chord. The Ponte often appears at the beginning of a B section of a short bipartite composition; at that point, it makes musical sense to stay away from the tonic and build expectation for its return. Example

EXAMPLE 11.14   Romanesca bass and example from Loeillet.

EXAMPLE 11.15   Romanesca/Prinner combination in two voices and a stylistic realization.

11.16 shows the B section of Leopold Mozart's Minuet in F in which a Ponte occupies the first four measures. The Ponte may be formed out of any kind of figuration (chords, single notes, busy arpeggios) as long as the prevailing harmony is V, and the passage communicates a sense of tarrying.

EXERCISE: Develop a collection of passages and figurations that allow you to tarry on a dominant. These need not be virtuosic. When you are confident, improvise complete pieces over the template in Example 11.11, replacing the Fonte with a Ponte. Play in various keys and meters.

The Tonic-Dominant Oscillation (TDO) may occur in various inversions of both chords. The TDO has many applications and may serve as an opener, continuation, or tarrying device. As the name implies, the schema simply moves back and forth between I and V. Example 11.17 shows a minuet from Loeillet's Suite in G minor, beginning with a Do-Re-Mi, Prinner, followed by a TDO.

EXAMPLE 11.16   Example of a Ponte from Leopold Mozart.

EXAMPLE 11.17   Loeillet: Do-Re-Mi/Prinner/TDO. J. C. Bach: TDO.

Next in the same example is an excerpt from J. C. Bach's Sonata in A, Op. 17 no. 5, with a rather ambitious TDO.

EXERCISE: Practice TDOs in many keys, first in block chords and then with stylistic keyboard techniques. Write down your best ideas in your zibaldone. When you are confident in your ability, improvise a complete piece using the template from Example 11.11 but employing a TDO in place of the Do-Re-Mi. You could also replace the Fonte with a TDO, but the TDO should be transposed so that the chords are V and V/V. In this case, near the end of the TDO you will need to modulate back to the original key.

The *Monte* ("mountain") is a schema that climbs chromatically in the bass. It communicates a sense of energetic climbing as it tonicizes ever higher chords. The Monte may provide a pathway to a new tonal area such as the mediant, or it may initiate a dramatic return to the tonic. Like most schemata, its applications are flexible.

Its first stage is a secondary dominant in first inversion, resolving in the second stage to a root-position triad. It then repeats this pattern. The second and fourth (and possibly sixth) stages are on strong beats. However, if each stage of the schema occupies a full measure, the placement of perceived strong and weak locations is less important. In major keys the most common version follows ③-④-♯④-⑤ in the bass, with secondary dominants of both IV and V.

I bet you hated reading the previous paragraph as much as I hated writing it. This is an example of something that is almost impossible to understand in words, but is quite easy at the keyboard. Once you work through the exercises, I promise that Montes will not be so bad.

The longest major-key Montes start on ③ in the bass and conclude on ⑥, making a six-stage schema ending on the relative minor. Even though chromatic movement in the bass cannot proceed past ⑥ (because nobody uses secondary dominants of the leading tone), the bass may continue rising diatonically to ①, completing the arrival at the tonic. In this case the schema "ends" at ⑥ (because the bass no longer moves chromatically), but since ⑦-① also take dominant and tonic chords respectively, the last two chords will sound like they are part of the schema.

One may also create a Monte with ♯①-②-♯②-③, ending on iii. In this version, the first two stages of the schema are indistinguishable from those of a Fonte.

Because each stage of the Monte appears to modulate to a new key area, we describe the soprano not with scale degrees but as intervals above the bass. Most commonly the soprano will include a diminished fifth above the bass on each dominant chord, resolving to a third on the following root position chord. These major-key versions, along with Montes from Haydn's Sonata in C♯ minor, Hob. XVI/36, and C. P. E. Bach's Rondo No. 2, Wq. 56, appear in Example 11.18. The Haydn follows ♯①-②-♯②-③, and the Bach follows ③-④-♯④-⑤-♯⑤-⑥. Note that although the Haydn is from a minor-key sonata, this particular section is in a major key.

EXAMPLE 11.18   Monte examples from Haydn and C. P. E. Bach.

In minor keys a Monte is possible on #③-④-#④-⑤, as well as ⑤-⑥-#⑥-⑦-#⑦-①. Example 11.19 demonstrates both Montes, with selections from the Scherzando movement of Haydn's C♯ minor sonata, Hob. XVI/36, and Cimarosa's Sonata in C minor. Note that the minor schemata use the same notes (but not the same scale degrees) as the major versions.

EXERCISE: Practice Montes in all versions as described in previous paragraphs, and in a variety of keys. Start with simple, two-voice outlines, then fuller block chords, and finally with stylistic keyboard techniques.

EXERCISE: Using the template from Example 11.11, replace the Fonte and Indugio with a six-stage Monte. Figure out how to connect the Monte with the final cadence. Improvise over this plan in several keys.

We learned the Quiescenza in the chapter on figuration preludes. The Quiescenza may function as an opener and was among J. S. Bach's favorite starting moves. It may also serve as a kind of postscript after the final cadence, "sealing" the harmonic arrival in the tonic. The Quiescenza employs a pedal point on ① in the bass, with two upper voices articulating some form of V7/IV-IV-V (or vii°)-I. Example 11.20 shows an abstract outline of a Quiescenza together with the opener and postscript from the Prelude in C from Book II of J. S. Bach's *Well-Tempered Clavier*. Interestingly, this piece uses the Quiescenza as both beginning and ending.

EXAMPLE 11.19 Minor Montes from Haydn and Cimarosa.

EXAMPLE 11.20 Quiescenza examples from J. S. Bach.

EXERCISE: Review the Quiescenza in several keys. Improvise over the template from Example 11.11, replacing the Do-Re-Mi with an opening Quiescenza, and adding extra measures to the end of the template (after the cadence) to accommodate a postscript Quiescenza.

Choose some short pieces by composers from the galant style. Look for schemata. Develop your own templates for improvising, and write them in your zibaldone.

Chapter 12

Resources for Further Study

We have covered only a small portion of the vast territory of historical improvisation. Because improvising musicians are intelligent and restless, you will probably want to keep learning. Still, you may find this journey difficult due to the lack of travel companions. In order to provide a virtual home for a community of improvisers, I have set up an online discussion forum where we can discuss this book, trade advice, and post videos of our improvisations. Visit www.johnmortensen.com to learn more.

To find a large collection of partimenti and historical treatises visit the website of Professor Robert Gjerdingen: http://faculty-web.at.northwestern.edu/music/gjerdingen/partimenti/index.htm.

The chapter on partimento discussed only a few introductory concepts. To continue in this area, I recommend studying Fenaroli's complete treatise *Regole Musicali* (*Rules of Music*). Gjerdingen has provided a translated (and legible!) version at his website. I consulted it frequently in writing this book.

Several websites have lists of schemata. If you do a search for "galant schemata," you will find them. Musicologist John Rice posts videos on YouTube under the name "settecentista." He has assembled audio examples of many schemata, editing together numerous examples of the same schema from a wide variety of repertoire. His videos provide a unique, enjoyable overview of the many ways composers deploy schemata.

Once I understood that improvisation is made of bass motions first, upper voices next, and diminutions like frosting on top, I began collecting bass motions in my zibaldone. I find that in most improvised concerts I do not use every bass motion I know. I tend to have several favorites bouncing around in my head at any given time. When I hear that my improvisations are relying too heavily on those favorites, I return to my zibaldone and restock my mind with new ideas. I suggest undertaking a long-term project to learn every bass motion you can, and keep track of them by writing them down.

The best resource for ongoing study is simply the repertoire itself. In writing this book, I have encountered many quandaries. (Do toccatas need a unifying theme? Are variations allowed to change meters? Under what circumstances does Bach write an augmented sixth chord?) Returning over and over to the original sources has always been rewarding. I suggest digging into the great composers, of course, but also the many lesser-known musicians of centuries past. Bach may be the best eighteenth-century composer, but for that very reason is not typical. Getting to know the work of average writers is useful as well; in historical improvisation we want to know not only what was exceptional, but also what was typical. And of course, some of those average composers occasionally jotted down real gems.

A lifetime of playing repertoire leaves you with a linear mind. To be sure, a good performance of a practiced, memorized piece is a worthy accomplishment. But it is also a linear accomplishment, since it is precisely the same task every time. All the notes, phrases, harmonic progressions, and the physical motions to create them unfold identically every time you practice or perform. I suspect that as a result, the performer's mind becomes optimized for the task of storing and recalling this voluminous information *the same way and in the same order.* This is ideal if you want to play memorized concerts of difficult composed music.

But it doesn't work very well if you want to make choices. The essence of improvisation is real-time decision-making, the navigation of an endlessly branching set of pathways. Improvisation is—here's a great word—*rhizomic,* resembling the spreading of roots underground. The mind optimized for the linear will balk at the rhizomic. You may have felt a sense of mental stuttering while working through the exercises in this book. Don't be discouraged; this is the feeling of the linear-to-rhizomic struggle.

You can't force tomato plants to grow by pulling on them, but you can encourage their growth with sunlight, water, and nutrients. The same is true of improvisation. Only patient practice—and plenty of it—will produce the results you want. I felt this linear-to-rhizomic struggle strongly when learning to improvise fugue expositions. I tried for a couple hours every day. I understood the theoretical principles very well, and could easily compose a fugue on paper, but my mind would constantly hesitate when I played in real time. After six weeks of no measurable progress, something changed. I didn't understand intervals better or have any new insight into fugues; I already knew those things. Somehow the task was just easier; the process of making real-time decisions felt effortless and fun.

The tomato plants were starting to sprout.

Glossary

Terms invented by the author are marked with an asterisk (*).

ANSWER The second voice to enter in a point of imitation.

APP* Alternating pedal point, an improvisation technique in which a moving line in the right hand alternates with a repeated note on ① or ❺ in the left hand.

APRILE An opening schema with ❶-❼-❷-❶ in the melody and ①-②-⑦-① in the bass.

BICINIUM A two-voice polyphonic texture consisting primarily of thirds and sixths.

C5 Circle of Fifths, a common harmonic progression in which the bass moves by falling fifths.

COMPOUND MELODY A single line implying two or more lines by means of leaps.

CONVERGING CADENCE A cadence in which the bass passes through ④ and ♯④ before arriving at ⑤.

DIMINUTION Groups of shorter notes that decorate or connect longer structural pitches.

DO-RE-MI An opening schema in which the melody rises ❶-❷-❸.

DOTTED DIMINUTION* Diminution placed near the end of the beat in order to emphasize a dotted or similar rhythm.

FAKE STRETTO* The technique of creating the sensation of stretto by placing entries of thematic material in various voices in rapid succession.

FONTE A schema with ①-♯①-②-⑦-① in the bass and various possibilities for the melody.

FXB* Fauxbourdon, a harmonic progression of successive chords of the sixth (or first inversion).

GRAND Short for grand cadence, a cadential schema with ③-④-⑤ in the bass.

HEMIOLA A rhythmic phenomenon in which six beats may be divided into either two groups of three or three groups of two.

HS* Hidden sequence, a harmonic pattern whose true nature is obscured by surface figuration.

INDUGIO A schema in which a predominant harmony is prolonged through vigorous rhythmic activity.

JUPITER An opening schema with ❶-❷-❹-❸ in the melody and ①-⑦-⑦-① in the bass.

LAMENTO RO* A form of rule of the octave in which descending ⑥ in the bass takes ♮❻ in an upper voice.

LDC* Long diminished chords, an improvisation technique of extending a passage of diminished harmony by repeating it with rhetorically-organized figuration.

MEASURED Any music with normal measures with an equal number of beats.

MEYER An opening schema with ❶-❼-❹-❸ in the melody and ①-②-⑦-① in the bass.

MONTE A schema with ①-♯①-②-♯②-③ or ④-♯④-⑤-♯⑤-⑥ in the bass.

P10* Parallel tenths, the motion of two voices moving together in major and minor tenths.

PAGE ONE* An opening schema with ①-①-⑦-① in the bass and tonic, supertonic, dominant and tonic harmonies in upper voices.

PARTIMENTO A pedagogical bass line used in the eighteenth century to train musicians.

PE* Patterned elaboration, an improvisation technique in which a simple harmony is extended through the use of consistent figuration.

PLAY & CONTINUE* An imitative technique in which the theme continues with new material as the answer enters.

PLAY & HOLD* An imitative technique in which the theme sustains a pitch as the answer enters.

PLAY & REST* An imitative technique in which the theme rests as the answer enters.

POINT OF IMITATION A contrapuntal technique in which two or more voices enter at different times with the same thematic material.

PONTE A schema which is a prolonged dominant harmony.

PRINNER A continuing schema with ④-③-②-① in the bass and ❻-❺-❹-❸ in the melody.

QUIESCENZA A schema with ❶-lowered ❼-❻-raised ❼-❶ in the melody and a tonic pedal in the bass.

RHYTHMIC ACTIVATION* A technique of creating a polyphonic texture without adding new pitches by breaking structural pitches into shorter notes.

ROMANESCA An opening schema with several possible dispositions but in all cases the bass descends beginning on ①.

RULE OF THE OCTAVE The eighteenth-century Italian system of harmonizing a scale in the bass.

SCALE MUTATION A chromatic alteration of the scale usually leading to a modulation.

SEQUENCE A musical structure in which all voices move by repeated identical patterns.

SIMPLE RO* Simple rule of the octave, a form of Rule of the Octave with only three voices.

TDO* Tonic-dominant oscillation, the harmonic motion of trading between tonic and dominant harmonies several times.

THEME In a point of imitation, the first voice to enter.

UMPADEEDA* A common eighteenth-century figuration pattern with the bass on the beat and two upper voices filling out the remainder of the rhythm.

UNMEASURED A musical style of the eighteenth century usually written in whole note chords which are to be freely arpeggiated and not counted metrically.

WNC* Whole note chords, the improvisation technique of arpeggiating chords in an expressive and rhetorical manner.

ZIBALDONE A book in which the serious musician pursues relentless self-improvement through writing, by hand, notes on musical phenomena.

Bibliography

Bach, Carl Philipp Emanuel, and William J. Mitchell. *Essay on the True Art of Playing Keyboard Instruments*. New York: Norton, 2000.

Bach, Johann Sebastian, August Wilhelm Langloz, and William Renwick. *The Langloz Manuscript: Fugal Improvisation through Figured Bass; Edition and Facsimile*. Oxford: Oxford University Press, 2007.

Callahan, Michael. "Incorporating Long-Range Planning Into the Pedagogy of Baroque-Style Keyboard Improvisation." *Music Performance Research*. http://mpr-online.net/Issues/Callahan%20FINAL%20120311.pdf.

Czerny, Carl, and Alice L. Mitchell. *A Systematic Introduction to Improvisation on the Pianoforte: Opus 200*. New York: Longman, 1983.

Erhardt, Martin, and Milo Machover. *Upon a Ground: Improvisation on Ostinato Basses from the Sixteenth to the Eighteenth Centuries*. Magdeburg: Edition Walhall, 2014.

Gjerdingen, Robert O. *Music in the Galant Style*. New York: Oxford University Press, 2007.

Gooley, Dana Andrew. *Fantasies of Improvisation: Free Playing in Nineteenth-Century Music*. New York: Oxford University Press, 2018.

Hamilton, Kenneth. *After the Golden Age: Romantic Pianism and Modern Performance*. Oxford: Oxford University Press, 2008.

Hancock, Gerre. *Improvising: How to Master the Art*. New York: Oxford University Press, 1994.

Ijzerman, Job. *Harmony, Counterpoint, Partimento: a New Method Inspired by Old Masters*. Place of publication not identified: Oxford University Press, 2019.

Overduin, Jan. *Making Music: Improvisation for Organists*. New York: Oxford University Press, 1998.

Rabinovitch, Gilad, and Johnandrew Slominski. "Towards a Galant Pedagogy." *Music Theory Online* 21, no. 3 (2015). doi:10.30535/mto.21.3.10.

Remeš Derek, and Robin A. Leaver. *Realizing Thoroughbass Chorales in the Circle of J.S. Bach*. Colfax, NX: Wayne Leupold Editions, 2019.

Ruiter-Feenstra, Pamela. *Bach & the Art of Improvisation*. Ann Arbor, MI: CHI Press, 2011.

Sanguinetti, Giorgio. *The Art of Partimento: History, Theory, and Practice*. New York: Oxford University Press, 2012.

Schwenkreis, Markus. *Compendium Improvisation: Fantasieren Nach Historischen Quellen Des 17. Und 18. Jahrhunderts*. Basel: Schwabe Verlag, 2018.

Spiridion a Monte Carmelo. *Nova Instructio pulsandis organis, spinetti, manuchordiis*. Colledara: Andromeda Editrice, c 2003.

Strobbe, Lieven, David Lodewyckx, and Hans Van Regenmortel. *Tonal Tools: For Keyboard Players*. Antwerpen: Garant Publishers, 2014.

Tour, Peter Van. *The 189 Partimenti of Nicola Sala*. Uppsala: Uppsala Universitet, 2017.

Index

Exercise are indicated by *ex* followed by the page numbers